# I was looking for Love
## Powers on the earth

Bianca Grootfaam

Highly Favored Publishing
The Netherlands

**I was looking for love: Powers on the earth**
1st edition
©2015 by Bianca Grootfaam.

*The Holy Bible, King James Version.* Cambridge Edition: 1769; *King James Bible Online*, 2015. www.kingjamesbibleonline.org. Used by permission.

Editing by Eunice Anita, Duvilène Pieter and Tairina Waoe
Cover illustration © 2015 by Highly Favored Publishing
Book Layout © 2014 by BookDesignTemplates.com

Published by Highly Favored Publishing
www.highlyfavored.nl

*Some names and identifying details have been changed to protect the privacy of individuals.*

*Because of the dynamic nature of the Internet, any web addresses or links contained in this book may have changed since publication and may no longer be valid.*

*The views expressed in this work are solely those of the author and do not necessarily reflect the views of the publisher.*

**True Story**
Paperback ISBN 978-94-92266-01-9
E-book Mobi ISBN 978-94-92266-05-7
E-book Epub ISBN 978-94-92266-06-4
NUR 402, 700

# Dedication

*I dedicate this book to The Almighty God because*
*He gave me the grace to write it.*
*Thank you Father for blessing me with a man as Dayan.*
*Thank you that we can preach Your Word,*
*praise and worship You together.*

# CONTENT

# INTRODUCTION

I t was a cold and quiet evening. I was laying on my bed in a cell of the Nsawam female prison in Ghana thinking of some of the things I had wanted in my life. I have wanted to write my story for a long time, but it was my Bible school teacher, Dan Buxton, who inspired me to actually do so. When he had told me to do so, I thought why not? I had been arrested for the third time and it was about time to wake up and find out where the roots of my problems lay.

That night I decided to ask for a pen and a piece of paper to write some points down. These points would become the start of the text for a book, this book. I wrote while I was in prison. For me being able to do so, I had to request permission of the Officer In Charge (OIC) who is the director at the facility. Inmates were not allowed to have paper and pencils or pens but I needed those in order to write my story. I received the permission under the condition that I would submit my notes for a review by the OIC. I had no problem with the limitation as long as I could write my story.

I started to write and while doing so, I wanted the whole world to know that I was writing. Once finished, I handed the material over to the OIC as we had agreed beforehand. After some days she came to me and she had tears in her eyes. She handed over my paperwork and told me that the story was very powerful, that it had made an impact on her and she was sure that it would impact others too. I thanked her for the compliment and stored the papers in the only place that was possible in the cell, under my pillow.

To my surprise a cellmate took my papers and read the story. After she was finished she gave me the following written reaction:
*Please Bianca, do not be ashamed of yourself. Say the truth and let the devil be ashamed. We are going to learn from your mistake and those who are coming behind, will learn something good from you. I know that if you do so, all the glory and honor will be for God because the Bible says that all "sins are sins" there is no big or small; starting from lying. Please do not be annoyed at me. It is just a piece of advice from a sister to a sister. Let your entire story be genuinely true, please forgive me, but I am saying it so that, you will correct your mistakes. Bianca, say it all and be free forever. If I had not been close to you, I wouldn't know how sweet you are.*

I had not requested feedback from a cellmate and initially I was annoyed that she took my stuff without permission. On the other hand, afterwards I was kind of happy with the feedback as it confirmed the words spoken by the OIC.

In your hands you have the final product after some editing and fine tuning of the text. Hopefully after you have finished reading my story, you will not make the same mistakes I did in the past. Even if you are doing them now, I hope you stop. I was ignorant back then and didn't know the Lord. Now, I want the whole world to know that no matter the situation, if you give your life to Jesus Christ, your situation will change.

Read my story and you will understand how come I am so certain about that. The story flows from my childhood to the choices I made as a teenager and as a young adult. You will get information about the consequences of my choices and the way I had operated in a chapter of my life which is now closed, closed forever.
In the last chapter I will provide information about the evil forces on this world that influenced my choices, my life and my way of living. Most important part of the last chapter is how to keep away and rebuke those evil forces from your life and from the life of your loved ones.

*My prayer for you is that the Almighty God will bless and protect you all the days of your life. That you become (more) aware of the fact that you have the choice to choose for Jesus and the love and protection that only He can offer. That the Holy Spirit may guide you and the angels of God protect you while you are reading this book. That you will not focus on judging me, my attitude and choices made, but that you will become aware that behind every choice there are invisible forces, spiritual forces, and that protection from the evil forces comes only from the Holy Trinity: Father, Son and Holy Spirit.*

Once I was looking for love. Now, in Jesus, I have it all.

Blessings from the bottom of my heart,

Bianca.

# CHAPTER ONE

# MY CHILDHOOD

M y name is Bianca Grootfaam and I wrote the basic text for this book, in my late thirties. I was born and raised on the west side of Amsterdam, the capital of The Netherlands. My parents are originally from Suriname, which lies in South America. Your background might be different from mine but surely you will be able to relate to or understand the circumstances described in this book and their consequences. It all started in my childhood.

*My early years*

When I think about my youth, I can say that I was intensely and desperately looking for love. My father was, as he would call himself, a business man. He was never at home which made me very sad. At that time he was a drug dealer and most of the time he was absent during the day and the evening. I saw him most of the time at dawn, when I went to the bathroom to do my needs and made use of the opportunity to take a look at him while he was sleeping. I used to steal money out of his pocket while he was sleeping.

As he had a lot of cash, he did not notice that some money was missing or at least, he never complained about it to my sister or me. Around the time that my mother used to wake my sister Mariska and me up for us to take our bath as preparation to go to school, dad would be either sleeping, factually snoring, or he would had left already. There was no opportunity for a *good morning pa*" or a hug for my sister and me in the morning hours.

Mariska is the only sister I have and she is eleven months older than me. My mother would walk Mariska and me to the kindergarten, and later on to the primary school, as it was a walk of only 5 minutes. Our mother was the one in charge of preparing our meals lunchboxes for school but sadly enough, she did all of this with little love. We would open our lunchboxes at school and we would notice that the bread had a green color on the inside because of the filling. The filling was green cheese, each and every day green cheese. This cheese gets its color and name from the herbs and spices that it is made of. It is an expensive cheese, but as child you want sandwich with children favored delicacies such as chocolate spread or luncheon meat. Above all, you want sandwich that is prepared with love.

During those years there was little to no happiness in my mother's life. My father was a handsome man and the ladies liked him a lot. On his turn, he gave them attention with all the consequences thereof. All of this gave my mother feelings of bitterness, jealousy and all you can imagine in those kinds of situations. As their marriage did not change for the better, my mother got to the point of serious depression. This situation led to the use of medication and maybe more substances during those days. She was so depressed during the early years of my life and the years that would follow that she could not give love to us. She became so attached to the use of her medications that one time she slept the whole day to the extent that she forgot to pick us up from school. My mother was so down in her feelings that she did not want to celebrate Christmas, birthdays, Mother's day or anything that would bring happiness to the family.

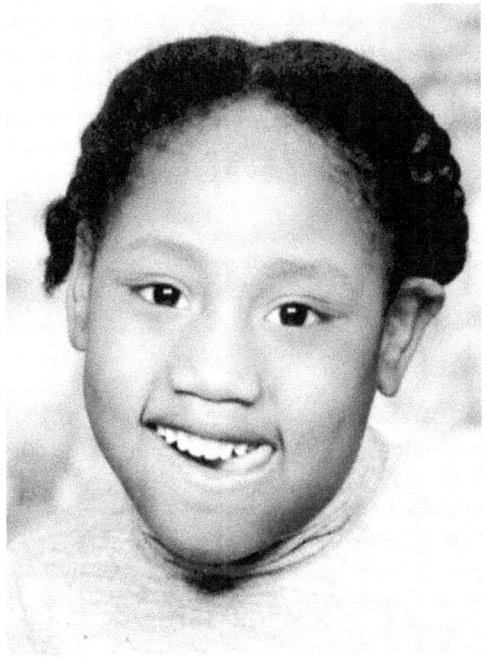

*Bianca at age 6*

She did not pay much attention to us. She did not even teach me how to cook or clean the house, and the lack of the aforementioned abilities had a very bad influence on my marriage. I will elaborate on my marriage and all that was related to it in chapters 3 and 4.

Up to this day (the time when I wrote the basic text) the wounds of the past in my mother's heart are not healed completely. When reflecting on my childhood, it was as if all seemed hopeless and because of that, my sister Mariska was never happy with herself.

> *Our parents gave us money but no love.*

### My grandmother and her contribution

My sister and I were raised by ourselves with a little help from our maternal grandmother, Grandma Cornelia. She was the sweetest grandma one could ever have. She used to come to the house every day, as she was so concerned about us, but sometimes my mother would not open the door for her. My sister and I would then cry because we wanted to see grandma. I remember very well that one time, on my birthday, grandma came by with a birthday cake, but my mother said that nobody should open the door. Grandma had no other option than to take the cake back home. That was very sad. Shortly said, our parents gave us money but no love.

I never saw my mother or my father, either praying or going to church. Consequently, I was not familiar with the beliefs and customs of a believer. The primary school I attended, which was located in the western part of the city, was associated with a Roman Catholic Church. Once in a while I would go to the church service, but I had no understanding of what was happening during the services. My grandmother was the one who taught my sister and me how to pray, to say 'The Lord's Prayer' and to have mercy.

When eating at grandma's house, before eating we would say: "*Lord, bless this food. Amen*" and make the cross sign in the name of the Father, the Son and the Holy Spirit.

When we were a bit older, like 12 years old, I think grandmother was attending to the services of the Evangelic Brother Fellowship (official name: Evangelisch Broeder Gemeente). We would dress nice and go to the service to see if we could find a handsome boyfriend. Due to the aforementioned we (my sister and I) never listened to the preaching. Nonetheless, we enjoyed being there.

Although grandmother was attending the church, she believed in and practiced the fetish. She used to bathe us with flowers and drinks, especially on New Year's Day. When we were sick would her family, as we were told in order to help us, organize "cultural parties" where the people would dance and call upon spirits. This is what I experienced and learned about the life of a believer. Later on I learned, initially by looking for ways to change, what a true believer in Jesus is like.

## My education and talent

Throughout the years, the situation at home did not become better. My mother and my father used to fight very often and very violently. I can still remember one time, early in the morning, when my father had beaten my mother and she had hit him as well. I went on hiding under the bed because I did not want to see how they would harm each other. It was so horrible and frightening. I did not want to lose my mother nor my father because of a fight. I used to wet my bed and also sack on my thumb, both more as an expression of my fear than as incompetence.

At the age of 13 years, I began skipping school, and roam in the streets of East Amsterdam, simply because I could not concentrate at school. When I was in the classroom, I would think about what would be going on in the house. At that time I attended a school in the east part of Amsterdam. I really lived in fear and trauma. I was so scared and felt bad emotionally, yet I never told anybody about this. I needed to live, have a life with stability, union, love, but my parents could not provide it for me. Because of the aforementioned, I preferred to accompany some of my classmates to their homes and neighborhood instead of going home.

We attended school in East Amsterdam but most of my classmates lived in Amsterdam-Southeast, the so called Bijlmer area. I went on roaming the streets in East Amsterdam more frequently, having fun with my friends, going out to clubs and having many boyfriends. My mother used to beat me every day; if it was not for wetting my bed, then it was for arriving home late.

When I think about the way I was, I can only say that God really loved me and still loves me. I used to walk late at night in the streets, having several boyfriends who could have given me diseases. Despite of the attention given to me on the streets, I had an unsatisfied feeling. I felt sad most of the time. When I was sad, I used to listen to my father's long plays containing songs of Carla Thomas including *'No pain no gain'* or *'If you should lose me you lose a good thing'*. I also listened to Surinamese songs and there was one song that I loved very much. It was a song of Eddy Hasang titled *'Mi jere fu ding tra wang dat you na wang waka mang'* which means I heard that you are a man of the street. Listening to music made me feel at ease. I loved music from the age of five. At the primary school I found out that I could sing and from that time on I was interested in singing. During those early years, my mother and my father had not supported me in anything because they were too busy with themselves. Years later, every time this discussion would come up, they would argue that the lack of attention towards me was because of the fact that I used to roam in the streets after school.

One time, that was in Amsterdam-Southeast, to be exact in the neighborhood called Kraaiennest, I was sitting outside while no one of my age was around. It was around 8 o'clock in the evening; it was already getting dark. I was about 13 years old. A lady was walking by and when our eyes crossed each other, she stopped. She kept looking at me and spoke to me by saying: *"Hey little girl, I want you to go home. Where are your parents?"* I stuck my thumb in my mouth and just looked at her. My attitude did not scare her off and she asked me to accompany her. I did not known her but still I responded to her request by standing up and walking in the direction she was heading in. She took me to her place and once there she asked me for my mother's telephone number. I was scared for my mother's reaction so I gave her my grandmother's phone number instead. It was already 10 o'clock when the lady called grandma that night. They had a nice talk based on the words I heard her speaking, her expression and voice tone. I think that afterwards, grandma called my mother and told her that I was with her in order to cover for me.

That night I stayed at the lady's house. Her name was Diana Blijd and she was very nice to me. She asked me several questions upon which I responded. She even asked why I didn't want to go home. Once I had answered this question, she stretched her arms towards me, hugged me and told me that it was okay. She gave me a clean set of sleepwear for me to put on and a cup of tea. The atmosphere was nice and warm; way different from what I was used to. Once I was ready, she guided me to the bedroom where I could stay for the night; a bedroom for me alone. As I lay down on the bed, I covered myself with the bed cover and fell asleep soon. I woke up the next morning, took a shower, had breakfast and headed to school. That afternoon I went home because I had to change my clothes. After this day I stayed in contact with Mrs. Blijd.

Because I was regularly in her neighborhood, I paid her some visits. Sometimes I even (mis)used her hospitality and stayed over for the night. On those occasions, when she asked me if my parents knew where I was, I told her to just call my grandmother to inform her. I really enjoyed the conversation moments the two of us had. It was during one of these conversations that I learned that she was an organizer of youth events. To be more precise, she used to gather talented youth and train them in arts like playing musical instruments, singing and modelling. Furthermore she arranged shows where young people were able to show their talents. Her work was mainly aimed at keeping the youth out of the streets. She worked a lot at the center called Bontekraai in the neighborhood Kraaiennest of the Amsterdam-Southeast area.

I found the work of Mrs. Blijd very appealing and interesting because I was very interested in the art of singing. At the primary school I participated once in a song festival organized by the teachers and I won the first price. I told Mrs. Blijd all of this and she invited me to participate at the activities at the Bontekraai instead of staying out on the streets. I took her offer and soon after I was almost every day at the center. I took modeling lessons, participated in shows where we had to show clothing at events and I also participated in the choir. The choir was very active with giving presentations.

I remember that one time on Christmas when we gave a performance at the jail in Amsterdam. Mrs. Blijd was very professional. One time she got a contract for a performance for the choir in a new television program in Italy. All the members of the choir had to request permission of their parents to participate in the show, especially because some travelling was involved. I went to my parents and requested for them to sign the required paperwork. Sadly enough, I had to wave the choir members out and see the bus drive away because I had no permission to participate; my mom refused to let me participate. Despite this disappointment, I look back at this period as a period in which Mrs. Blijd tried to give me some of the basic aspects that I needed in my life which I had lacked of.

The training I received from Diana had given me more confidence for my performance on stages. Some acquaintances of mine who knew that I could sing well, invited me to be part of their band. We were more or less of the same age, the age of 14. We were a band consisting of four girls and people used to call one of the girls the name of Chaka Kan because of her hair style. One song we loved to perform was titled '*You don't have to tell me*'.

I can't remember now who the original singer of that song was. Each of us had a solo part when performing the song and in 1988 we traveled around major neighborhoods in Amsterdam to give performances. Then it came to a point where I got an opportunity to add another level to my singing career.

My sister had a friend who could sing like it is no man's business. She asked me one day if I wanted to participate in a song festival. However, this song festival was meant for adults. I had a big posture for my age of fourteen therefore I looked much older. We thought it would not be obvious that I am too young to participate. On the other hand, there was my mother and her opinion. I wanted to participate so badly, but I knew that my mother would never allow me. I was sure about that because of an incident that had taken place before. There was a time that the Caribbean people had a carnival activity and they had asked if Chaka Kan, Sas (the nickname of another group member) and I could come and sing. We went to the event as agreed but I did not inform my mother about it. My mother was at home that evening and around 7 o'clock she asked my sister where I was. Once she knew where I was, she came there and beat the hell out of me in the presence of everybody. I was so ashamed.

Let us go back to the song festival. Like I mentioned earlier I was thinking whether to participate or not, considering what had happened at the carnival activity. Singing had always been my passion so I decided to participate while being fully aware that it could mean that I would get beaten up every day. Despite the odds, my friend and I decided that I would go the next day to register for participation in the song festival. That evening I couldn't sleep.

I do not recall who organized the song festival but I do remember that there were flyers and posters announcing the song festival at almost all the bus stops in the neighborhood Ganzenhoef. The selection rounds were held at the music studio Melody Line and the final was scheduled to take place at another location in Ganzenhoef. The next morning I went bodily to the studio and registered myself for the song festival. I was told that the next time I should bring 50 guilders and a master tape so that the band could play the music I wanted. The days went by and the day on which the first preliminary would be held arrived. There were like 50 participants and one had to sing till the final five were chosen. I thought I would not make it through because of my figure and for the fact that I am a woman.

Despite all, I managed to stay in the contest for two weeks and every day I received a beating from my mother. We had to be in the studio at 6 o'clock in the evening and that was the time for us to go to bed according to my mother's rule. Consequently, during those two weeks, I arrived home late based on the house rules. Every time my mother had beaten me, I said in my heart: *"I will sing, even if I have to die!"* That is the love I had and still have for music. For the final day of the contest, which would take place on the Friday evening, I decided the night before to run away from home. I bought myself a nice denim skirt with a black corset top and some black pumps and I went to Diana's place. Diana was not at home but she had told me earlier how I could get in and wait for her inside. Once I realized that, it was the week that Diana would not be in town, I decided to stay for the night at her home. I woke up the next morning and I was ready for the final.

I made my arrangements and arrived very early at the place where the contest would be held, way before six o'clock. I went to the dressing room to wait for the time to come that the finalists would be called up for the performances. I noticed that the jury for that day consisted of three matured and well-known persons. I knew that people called one of them Bem and another one was a woman who was a singer  of the band called 'Oema Soso'. The jury called the participants one by one for the final performances. I was the third person that was called and I sang '*Many rivers to cross*' and '*A woman in love*'. When I finished singing, I went back to the waiting room.

I was very nervous, so nervous that sweat was running all over my body. I was nervous because I had run away from home and it was getting very late. I think it was around midnight by then, but the only question that was circulating in my mind was: Am I going to win? I was peeping at the people sitting in the audience to see if I knew somebody, but they were mainly adults and none looked familiar to me. Some friends of mine were present but I was not able to spot them in the audience. Once all the 5 finalists had the chance to perform, there was a pause. After a while the judges finished with their counting and ranking of the participants and they proceeded to announcing the prizes. They started with the third place. The name of the finalist was mentioned and the concerning person walked towards the stage to receive the price. Then I heard them calling my name. I was so nervous to come out, that the host took me by one hand and guided me to the platform while in her other hand she held the cup for the second place. I won. Not the ultimate price, the first place, but a second place which was not bad at all.

Once the contest was over, some of my friends who were present and had cheered for me came to me to congratulate me. I was so glad but at the same time I was afraid that my parents would beat me up when I arrived home. I told my friends that I had ran away from home and one of them offered for me to stay at her home because she knew that her mother would not mind for a couple of days.

The next day, Saturday, I woke up at the house of my friend's family. She had just asked her mother for me to stay over because it was weekend. I could borrow clothing and we had a wonderful day. In the evening we went to a dance competition in the neighborhood and to my own surprise I won a price at that competition too. This price was even worth a mentioning in the local newspaper. As we had a new accomplishment to celebrate for, I stayed that night too at my friends'. My mother realized on the Sunday that I had not been home for three days and she told my father who started to search for me. My sister contacted some of my friends and they found out where I was. My father and my sister came to pick me up at my friend's house. At the time I got home, my dad told me that he didn't know that I could sing that well. Despite the positive comment I received a round of beating from my father for the fact that I had ran away. This time the beating was more than justified.

The reaction of my mother was as usual. After all, it worked out well. I was back at home with my family hoping that it would continue to be fine but it was sadly enough for a short, very short period.

*Bianca performing at the primary school song festival*

# CHAPTER TWO

# YOUNG AND LIBERAL

My mother continued to be full of anger, bitterness and stress. She was so stressed, that grandmother took us, my sister and me, to live with her. The situation became just too harsh for her to sit and watch from the sideline.

Grandma, or Granny as I used to call her, was always lovely and when she drank two cans of Heineken, she became happier. She used to drink her portion of Heineken around six o'clock in the evening which is the time she sat down to watch the news followed by the Sesame Street program. She finished the round with the television soap the Bold and the Beautiful.

She always gave us something nice to eat. She was very good and we could talk about anything with her. From small talks about the weather, to life issues, such as whom our friends are and who we were dealing with.

It was after moving in with granny that I experienced my first pregnancy. Though I had moved in at granny, I had not changed my lifestyle. I got pregnant by a guy named Bernard who had loved me a lot. Because I was so young, I was only 15 years old, I went for an abortion and only granny knew about it.

I was laying in the hospital in Amsterdam and the nurses were nice to me. The nurse put a cup on my nose for the anesthesia and I was gone. By the time I woke up, I was in a room with several other women around me. They were still sleeping, because they had had an abortion too. Bernard's mother called me the next day to ask me if it was true that I was pregnant. I told her that I just had aborted the baby and when Bernard became aware of this, he felt I had betrayed him and ultimately he ended our relationship that same year.

### *Parties and more parties*

The fact that Bernard broke up our relationship, did not bother me for long for I had other activities to keep my mind busy. One of them was my performances as part of a singing group. There were two girls in my class that were part of a singing group and without any specific reason that I was aware of, they asked me if I would like to join them. I started singing with them in 1987 and I continued doing that till mid-1989. So actually, when Bernard broke up with me, I just went on putting more efforts into the singing.

It was a group that used to sing Surinamese fetish music and also present theatrical plays. It was very interesting because we used to go from city to city and people who organized cultural parties contracted us for performances at their parties. We usually went to the parties to sing and drum. That was a timeframe in my life path in which I was going out a lot; back then I was a real party animal. In that season of my life, I frequently went to a place called Aboni, where old school music of party labels such as Otis Reading,

Sheena Easton and other songs in their genre were played on a regular basis. It was all slow music meant for adults but I was there. I was too young for such a place, but still I was there. Because I looked much older than I actually was, I was not questioned at the entrance or inside the building.

On an occasion that I was at that location, I wanted to buy some food. I was so focused on my walk towards the kitchen and I was not paying much attention to my surroundings, I just wanted to make a way through. Maybe I did not pay enough attention or an unexpected move was made by someone; I am not sure which one it was. The end result was that I pushed a guy and the glass he was holding in his hand made a non-natural movement leading to some spots on his shirt. Ouch! I could not help to think immediately *"This guy is going to beat me"* because I was used to getting beaten up whenever I had done something wrong. Amazingly, he didn't. He grabbed my hand and said: *"Can you look where you are going?"* I replied with: *"I am sorry sir. It won't happen again."* He was so handsome and hand a fair complexion. He had short hair; he was not too tall and had a nice deep voice. He looked at me and said: *"The next song, you will dance with me and then I will forgive you."* I was like okay, this is better than to get beaten up. The dance became my first dance with a 'real man'. I had danced before, but with boys of my age. He smelled so good and was nothing like the former boyfriends I had. Those boyfriends were kids just like me. Surely, this was a real man. He whispered in my ear: *"I will drive you home"*. His remark scared me because of what grandma would say if she saw me arriving with him, because I had left home with my friends.

Despite of these thoughts, I told him it was okay. He brought me home, but I requested him to park his car one street away from grandma's house. He gave me his business card, told me to come the next day to his café-bar, gave me a kiss on my forehead and once I stepped out of the car, he left. I walked towards home, went up the stairs and found that my sister was still awake. I told her that I had found the man of my life and that she should accompany me the next day to his bar. I read the name of the bar on the card and his name, Vernon, was also written on the card.

> *I hadn't mind her or her opinion,*
> *because*
> *I was looking for love.*

### *My first job*

We dressed up the next day a bit nicer than usual and headed for school. Once school was out, we took the bus and went to the address indicated on the card I received the day before from Vernon. It was a ride of approximately 20 minutes to the location, being a marketplace, as the school we were attending and the marketplace were located in Amsterdam-East. This is one of the marketplaces where the weekly open air market is held and it is located in the middle of a shopping area. In that area there were a lot of shops and cafés. We arrived at the market, stepped out of the bus and went on looking for the exact location stated on the card. Once located, we entered the café-bar and noticed that all the people that were inside, looked like men who could be our dad's friends. Vernon saw us and called me behind the bar and showed me how to tab the beer, serve the people and how to wrap up ganja indian hemp. My sister went on to sit at a table and wait for me.

After the first visit to the café-bar, I went there every day after school in order to work as I was instructed. I liked the job very much. Along the way my mum heard that I was working in the bar and she warned me that if I went there one more time, she would beat me. I hadn't mind her or her opinion, because I was looking for love. I finally found someone who was giving me attention and that felt good. My mother couldn't give it to me, so I felt that she should leave me alone.

Vernon was good to me. He took me out, gave me money but he didn't take advantage of me by kissing me or sleeping with me. I asked him one day if he really loved me upon which he replied: "*Of course*". I continued by asking him how come he was not sleeping with me and he told me that I should not rush in life. The conversation went on as I told him that I was not a virgin anymore whereupon he replied: "*The guy who has been sleeping with you isn't rational. You are too young.*" I told him: "*I am a big girl now, so I can handle it.*" He looked at me for a long time, and then, he kissed me and he said that he would think about it. The next day he brought me to a hotel where he had sex with me, but not much later I could see on his face that he felt guilty. That was the only time he slept with me. After 2 weeks of our one-nightstand, I got the same feelings I had with my first pregnancy. I knew I was pregnant but I didn't know how to tell him.

The next day after the discovery, I went to work as usual and I was singing while I was cleaning up and washing the glasses. The song that I was singing was one of the cultural songs that I had learned from the group I was part of. As Vernon heard me singing, he asked me how come I knew that song. He said: "*A little girl like you. Who taught you such songs?*" I proudly told him that I was a member of a cultural group and I said the name of the group. I saw how the color of his face changed immediately. I rushed to ask him what was wrong. He recovered very quickly, looked straight at me and asked me to mention the names of the members of the group. My favorite friend in the group was Vanessa so her name was the first one I mentioned. Upon my answer, Vernon looked at me angrily and said: "*So you knew that I have a wife!*" I was shocked by the statement he just made and all I was able to say was: "*Your wife?*" as I had a lot of questions going on my mind. He yelled at me to get out of his shop and to never come back again. I started to cry and then I told him that I was pregnant with his child. He said that the baby was not his and called me a prostitute. He continued by saying: "*I have heard about you. Go and abort it. If you don't, I will make sure you will be in a wheelchair for the rest of your life.*" I left the bar and headed home; alone and all by myself.

I left home the next morning and went to the doctor to whom I told that I was pregnant and I didn't want an abortion. We talked for a while about my life and living circumstances. Once I was finished with my story, the doctor called one of the institutions in Amsterdam for teenage mothers to request assistance and support for me. He gave me the address of the institution and as soon as I left the doctor's practice, I headed for the institution. I remember well that there was a lady who took care of me upon my arrival at the institution. She was very friendly. She counseled me, showed me my room and instructed me to go to the social welfare in order to receive money for a new start in my life. I went to the social welfare and they gave me 1,000 guilders from which I bought baby items, pots, furniture, TV and all other things I needed. The next day I called Mariska and told her to tell mum and grandma that I was doing well and to inform them that I had my own place. After this, I didn't see my mum nor my dad for 8 months. During that time period, it was grandma who kept in contact with me and she took good care of me. I will never forget my grandma. I loved her so much.

Notwithstanding my pregnancy, I continued attending school because grandma told me that I should not quit school. I went to the school named De Werkruimte offered by the 'Pedagogisch Psychologisch Instituut', or as we used to call it the PPI School. There I followed classes on the MAVO-level which is equivalent to high school in Amerika and SHS Level in Africa. One day when I arrived at school, the teacher told me to go and sit in another classroom, alone and all by myself. This was around the 4th month of my pregnancy. I was wondering why they gave me some work to do but separated me from the group. It felt like they were punishing me. I was still asking myself what I had done wrong, when suddenly I heard: "*Surprise, Surprise!*" The whole school, teachers and students, entered the room with bags containing lots of baby items. May God bless all those people who stood by me during my pregnancy with gift items. They were so many that I did not need to buy anything else. Now I know that it was God who had seen my tears, he was my husband and my baby's father as He was the one who provided through those lovely people. This all took place in that same week of my birthday. Surprisingly, there was more surprise to come.

One night while I was watching TV, I heard the doorbell ring. I looked through the window and to my surprise it was my mum, dad, grandma, Mariska, aunt Siene and Uncle Glenn accompanied with a big pot of fried rice and drinks. It was so nice of them to visit me after such a long time and to have a lovely meal together.

## *My firstborn*

Time passed by and I reached the nine months of pregnancy. The baby would come soon. I remember very well that one morning, a lovely day in the month of June 1989, I went to the house of my friends Amy and Melody because I wanted to go with them to the market. I felt a heavy pain in my stomach but I disregarded it and we went to the market. The pain became heavier and heavier while we were at the market and as I told my friends that I could not bear the pain any longer, they accompanied me to the tram stop, entered the tram with me and brought me to a spot closer to my grandmother's house.

Upon our arrival at the tram stop close to my grandmother's house, we stepped out of the tram and I went on walking towards the house while my friends crossed the rails in order to take the tram and return to the market. When I reached the house, there was nobody and I realized that I was alone. I entered as I had the house key and I called every family member and acquaintances who I knew the phone number of and that I thought would be able to help me. Sadly enough, no one picked up their phone. As the pain was still heavy, I lay down on grandma's bed and for almost seven hours I was there alone and going through labor pain. Finally, grandma came home and when she saw me, she panicked but recovered quickly. Once again at her senses, she took me by the hand, brought me to her car and drove me to the hospital. Once the nurses took hold of me, Grandma had the chance to inform the other family members. Soon my Mum, Mariska and other family members arrived at the hospital. At nine o'clock in the evening I gave birth to a handsome baby boy whom I named Chervino.

As the medical employee was in the process of cutting of the navel string, we received our first non-family visit. Vanessa the wife of Vernon, still unaware of the relationship of the baby with her family, stepped into the room together with her sister. Once there was an opportunity, the sister of Vanessa picked up my baby, took a good look at him and said: "*This boy looks more like a Chinese and does not look like us.*" By referring to us, she meant people with a Suriname background. I replied by saying: "*It does not matter because I am his mother and his father.*" I was still bleeding because only a couple of minutes had gone by since I had given birth to my son. Considering my condition, my mum decided to give Vanessa and her sister five minutes to leave the room. She spoke to Vanessa and had finalized her sentence with the words "*if not …*".

When Chervino was about one month, my sister Mariska came to my apartment to pick us up with her car. When I spoke earlier that day with her, she said that we had to go and show the baby to Vernon. After some thinking I agreed with her and we went to the place where I used to work for Vernon. When we were approaching the café-bar, we noticed that the car of Vernon was parked in the middle of the road and the music was turned on very loud.

He was hanging with one arm out of the window. My sister parked her car on a parking spot close to Vernon's car. She stepped out of the car while I opened the door on my side. She took the baby from me and walked towards Vernon who was still in the car. I took my time to step out of the car and followed them slowly.

Vernon saw a shadow appear near him so he looked up at my sister and said: "*Welcome*". My sister spoke to him saying: "*I brought somebody for you to meet*". He took the baby from her, played a while with him and said: "*This child is a beautiful boy but he is not mine*". My sister became furious so she took the baby back, gave him to me and told me to go and sit in the car. All I did was follow her instructions. Once I was in the car, I turned to look at the scene outside and I noticed that my sister had pointed out two of her fingers on Vernon and was telling him a couple of things. I heard her say to him: "*As long as you don't accept this baby, nothing will go well in your life*". After this my sister came to the car and we drove away. Before a month had passed since our last encounter with Vernon, we heard that his wife had left him and his business was not going well. Ultimately, he got addicted to cocaine and his life became miserable.

> *...if all of us had known the Lord, as I know Him today, we wouldn't have made such mistakes*

*I always had a forgiving heart*

Regardless of all I had been through, I felt no hatred and still do not hate anyone. I had and still have a heart full of love. I understand everybody's situation and I don't blame anybody for anything. I believe that if all of us had known the Lord, as I know Him today, we wouldn't have made such mistakes. This is why I am able to forgive each and every one who had been in my life. This is now but back then, in the early 1990's, I was still looking for love.

*Bianca with her firstborn.*

# CHAPTER THREE

# LIFE AND DECISION MAKING

The lack of love in my childhood had driven me to search for love in the wrong places. My decision making process and my decisions were centered on what I thought was love. Soon after the birth of my first son, I rekindled my relationship with my old boyfriend who was the nephew of my friends Amy and Melody. I was not in love with him. We just had fun and out of fun, I got pregnant. This time I was not aware of the pregnancy at an early stage.

*I thought this is love*

In that same period of my life, my uncle Bally came over from Suriname and he stayed at grandma's house. He loved me a lot. One day a good friend of him came to visit him. They used to hang out together in the past and were very pleased to see each other again after a long time. My uncle introduced me to his friend, who I thought his name was Roy, and he suggested for us all together to go out that day. We went to the Aboni, the same club where I met

Vernon. My uncle's friend offered us some drinks and he rolled us some indian hemp. I noticed that for a while he kept looking at me. Suddenly, he turned to ask my uncle if he could have a dance with me and my uncle replied that it was no problem. He invited me to the dancefloor. Oh, my God! He was tall, black, handsome and smelled good. While we were dancing, he asked me: "*Why are you like that?*" I was surprised by the question so I asked him: "*What do you mean?*" He replied to me by saying: "*So you want to pretend. Take a good look at my face.*" Well, I looked up straight into his eyes and suddenly an incident of a couple of years before came into my mind. I remembered when I was 12 years old and I was walking somewhere in Amsterdam along a road and all of a sudden a car was following me. The driver had stopped his car near me and he had asked: "*Hey baby, what is your name?*" At that time I was somewhat scared, not familiar with boyfriends. So initially, I refused to talk to him but he kept on talking and convinced me to let him bring me home. Mum always taught us, that we should not enter the car of strangers because there were kidnappers who steal and kill children. As I knew the story of mum by heart, I told the driver to drop me off two streets before our house and I gave him my grandma's telephone number. That driver was now dancing with me in Aboni.

Back then, when I had given the telephone number to him, he found it strange because he recognized the number as the one that he used to call to reach my uncle. Now, after all those years, he saw me with my uncle and understood how come I gave him the telephone number of grandma's house. I explained to him that I had grown since our previous encounter and that I had a baby. I was happy when I was in his arms, and he finally got what he wanted. After this first date, he came to visit every day. We were so in love.

He invited me once again to go back to the club, but this time only the two of us. Once we entered the club, he asked me what I wanted to drink. I told him that I liked cocaine Remi Martel and as he turned towards the bar to place the order, something awkward happened; I fainted. The moment I woke up, I found myself lying in his arms at an unfamiliar place. It turned out that we were at his house. It would later turn out that at that time I was pregnant of my second born, but at that moment I was still not aware of the pregnancy. Obviously, my mate for that night was not the father. The next day, I warned the nephew of my friends, the father of mine unborn, not to come over again, because I was in love with someone else and didn't want to lose my boy.

Though I had my own place at the institution, I used to stay over at my grandmother's house, especially when going out at night because the baby would stay under the care of my grandma. One early morning staying at grandmother's place, I heard the phone ringing and I went to pick it up. Politely I said: *"Good morning, please who is on the line?"* The caller answered with: *"Good morning. My name is Tessa. Please, I am looking for Danny."* I responded: *"Please, I think you called the wrong line. I don't know anyone named Danny."* I heard her say: *"Oh"* and then she continued with: *"Or is Barry there?"* As she now had asked for my uncle, I said: *"Okay, wait a minute"*. I called my uncle and gave the phone to him, for him to continue talking with the lady. They talked shortly and as soon as my uncle had hanged the phone I asked him who this Danny was. He said to me: *"My niece, I can't tell you"* but I saw the expression on his face that he didn't want to hurt me. I did not ask for further explanation nor made other questions.

Later on that day, I went back to my own place. The man of my life, as I had in my mind at that time, came over in the late afternoon. While we were making love, I called him Danny. He was shocked and asked me immediately: *"How do you know my name?"* I answered: *"From your wife Tessa."* Upon my answer he began to beg me not to tell anything to his wife and he said some other stuff. I realized that he was not the kind of man that would have chosen for me. Shortly thereafter, I found out that he had many other intimate girlfriends. I was just one more. Once I knew that, I quit seeing him and ended our relationship.

In the meanwhile I found out about my current pregnancy. From that moment on, my focus went to my pregnancy and the son that I already had.

### *My second born*

With the coming of a second baby, some practical issues had to be resolved. My lodging, the room I had at the institution, would be too small for me and two kids and so the secretarial services at the institution made an appeal at the municipality in Amsterdam for me to get priority for allocation of a social house. Social houses in The Netherlands are houses or better said apartments that fit a family of 3 or 5 members that are build and rented by governmental institutions to individuals. The prices are subsidized by the government in order to keep it affordable for the people with lower incomes. The appeal was considered and within a short period of time I received the keys for a social house and I moved, with the help of family and friends, me and my son's stuff to our new accommodation. There I made the preparations for the birth of my second child. I paid the rent with the money I received from the social services because I received a social benefit on a monthly basis from the government. This social benefit is a benefit program The Netherlands has instituted to help individuals who do not have a job or are eligible for unemployment benefit. There are a fixed set of requirements that one should meet in order to receive this benefit. Once we were settled in our new home, my focus went on to my pregnancy.

A couple of months later, I gave birth to my daughter Janice. The baby was born sound and well. After four months, Janice's father came with his parents to my grandmother's and they asked me if they could have their grandchild. One way or the other, they knew that I was at my grandmother's on that particular day and at that time. Initially I refused, in fact I denied that he was the father, but he stood firm and said that the baby was his daughter upon which the grandfather pleaded to me if she could carry their last name. After a long thinking I agreed with the proposal. I have to admit that throughout the years they took good care of her. Whatever she needed, they provided it for her. May the Almighty Father bless that family. I never confessed to Danny that the baby was not his, and I thank God that he was not the father because he would have never taken care of Janice the way her father and his family did.


After the birth of Janice, I decided that I had to do something that would bring me and my children to a brighter future and improve our living conditions. With this in mind, I started with the education program for nurses at the nursery school in East Amsterdam. The program was a part-time study allowing the students to gain experience in the field while following the theoretical part of the program. The placement was mainly done by the school itself which made it easier for me. It is through this school that I received the opportunity to work at a nursery home and as I would be paid for working there, I did not have to depend on the social benefit anymore. I really enjoyed working with the elderly and being independent in the financial sense but it all went wrong at the end.

In the next two sections I will explain the reason why it went wrong.

## Another chance for love

There I was then, unmarried with two children in the early 90's. There was a gentleman who had stayed for a short while at my grandmother's house. He was a family friend and we called him Githy. I was not aware of the fact that my family had spoken to him about marrying me. Initially he showed no signs of interest or he was pretending. I don't know if it was coincidence, but he was, together with my grandma, at my side when I gave birth to Janice. I know my grandmother was thinking that it was enough. It should be over with those boyfriends and those matters. Githy was very nice to me. He bought me chocolates and gave me many flowers and presents. One day I invited him to my house.

Githy came over to my house and it was then when he asked me to marry him. He said: *"Do you want to marry me? I have talked to your family already and they are aware. In fact they were the ones who advised me to marry you, so you can help me with my nationality issues and I can take care of you and your kids"*. It was a good deal for me. Another chance for love and therefore I agreed.

We married on the 15th of March 1990 at a Roman Catholic Church in Amsterdam. My parents had taken care of the majority of the expenses and our wedding was celebrated with a nice party. There was a big and nicely decorated cake and a band playing live music. After this fantastic celebration, life as a married couple with 2 children began. From that moment on I started to call my husband Gilly. My children and I moved to the house of Gilly. Surely a mansion compared to our earlier tiny apartment. Even though we resembled a happy family, I was not happy in my marriage.

I couldn't forget about Danny and I was married to a man who was 15 years older. The most frustrated part was that we had sexual problems. Some of my friends had asked me, how it was possible to have sexual problems while we had all these children. In 1992 I gave birth to our daughter Channelta. In 1995 I gave birth to Chesteny and in 2000 I gave birth to Margillio. Believe me, I am the only one who can tell you and for sure the saying unless you have walked a mile in the shoe, was applicable in this case.

> *I was still looking for love and wanted to find a way in which I could have fun.*

*My choices*

From the time when I was a child I was looking for love. Once married, I thought that this search would have been over. The contrary was the case. The search continued. Why? I had everything. A husband, 5 beautiful kids, a nice house, a nice car and all I could have wanted in terms of material. Then again I was feeling empty. Something was missing in my heart. Our standard of living was fine as my husband earned enough with the trafficking of cocaine. We were living okay and still I missed something. What exactly? I was still looking for love and I wanted to find a way in which I could have fun.

In order to fill the emptiness, I decided to enter into the trafficking of cocaine as well. Did I have fun with this? Yes, I had. It was fun because I had my own money and I felt like the whole world was mine. My husband and I, had grown from trafficking drugs for others to having people carry it for us.

As indicated previously, I had a job at the nursery home as part of my education program to become a nurse. Due to the trafficking of drugs, I said a couple of times that I was sick and therefore not able to be present at work. This went on for some time but ultimately the curtains fell. Once my superiors got hold of my practices and the fact that I was lying about my health, I was fired. Consequently, I was not able to finish the education program. Back then I had little to no regrets that I had not finished the education program and not earned a degree because financially it was going very well for us.

Because we were both in this business, we used to visit native doctors, pa Eddy and pa Sammy. We would spend a lot of money with both of them in order to make sure we pass the controls at the airports. They would bathe us with different kinds of leaves and drinks, perform rituals including but not limited to killing of fowls, worshiping of shrines and they would also organize spiritual parties with bonga drums. They would continue with putting baskets with food and drinks on the water and push these to open water as payment to the gods (we called this payment of the rivers), burying eggs and also with making of medicine for us to rub on our body. They would even call our soul into a white (big) mug and ask it questions. I was so accustomed with the rituals, that I even started doing them by myself when I would find myself in a foreign country and I could not find a person like the pa's. I would then go to the bush, collect leaves and buy everything that we used to buy for the pa's.

I ended up bathing other people in accordance to the rituals indicated above. Whether or not it was the right thing to do, I did not know or think of at that time. All I know is that I did it!

It was in this period of my life that I began having affairs with a gentleman named Romeo. He was the love of my life and he always had time to listen to me. Minus point was that he too had a girlfriend. The relationship with Romeo was not enough for me at that time so I slept with many other men not realizing that I was destroying my body. I didn't know the value of my body.

## *I lost everything*

I was the type of person that trusted everybody and I didn't know that evil minded people existed. I had an acquaintance called Claire and another one called Serge. I knew the two of them through ciphered sources but because they used to come to my house we became very close. We used to play cards, go out together and have fun but the two of them where going through hardship. Knowing this fact, I introduced them to my cocaine business partner and we often went to Suriname together. We had a lot of fun and we all looked good by wearing expensive clothes with golden accessories, driving expensive cars, hosting big parties and so on. I brought them in contact with my friend Daisy and some other acquaintances in Suriname. We had some ups and also some downs, but because both my husband and I were in the business, we gained more money and we went on buying our own stuff. I didn't know that some people were jealous of us.

Life went on and one day I decided to buy a new complex of houses in Suriname. It was a new building project leading to a new era in the country. The complex was called Cocobiaco. Gilly and I went on talking with the seller and the man told us that he would fly the next day back to The Netherlands which meant that we could negotiate every arrangement there. We agreed with him to meet in The Netherlands for further negotiations. I told Claire and Serge that I had to return earlier to The Netherlands so I would leave them responsible for my cocaine, my money and the people who needed to transport the merchandise for me. Everything regarding my business was arranged and my husband and I left Suriname. What happened after this day turned my life upside down.

I don't remember very well, but I think it was on a Wednesday night, around 8 o'clock in the evening that it all started. My husband and I were watching TV when suddenly my phone rang. I picked it up and heard Claire screaming and crying on the phone. I said to her: *"Calm down! What is going on?"* She said: *"Armed robbers entered your house. They took all your money and the cocaine from us."* The cocaine we had lost was worth a lot. In fact my husband was furious and he wanted to kill the evildoers. On top of it, the two ladies that were on their way to The Netherlands, our last hope, were denounced by the same people. They had informed the police at the Amsterdam airport that two ladies coming from Suriname were carrying cocaine with them and after a severe control, our transporters were arrested. We lost everything. We were so sad. I told my husband not to worry and that we would start from scratch again. At that time I had the responsibility for six children as my stepdaughter Jenny, had just moved in with us. I had promised her a bright future, so she left Suriname with hope to step into a better life but that new life started to scatter piece by piece.

### *From a frying pan into the fire*

After the drop back, my husband and I made a trip to Curaçao, Dutch Caribbean. We stayed there for 2 weeks in order to pack a new transport of cocaine to The Netherlands. We took our baby, Margillio, with us but we left the other five children alone at the house. We did not request assistance of an adult for the children in the Netherlands, which was absolutely wrong. Our financial state, at that point in time, was just horrible. Take notice that as easy as the money was coming in, as easy it was given out. The moment that the setback came, there was no financial back-up. Simply said, in that situation we took strange decisions.

The dealers came to us on the day that we were about to travel back to The Netherlands and gave us the package that we should transport. We met at the hotel, but in a different room than the one that we were staying in. We made the arrangements with them after which the reception desk was requested to arrange a taxi to the airport for us. The taxi came to pick us up and we left the hotel. On the way to the airport, there was a surprise. One of the packages that was fitted on my body dropped down to my ankle. I told Gilly what had happened in a secretive way in order not to create any suspicion by the taxi driver. Gilly understood the situation immediately, and requested the taxi driver to turn back to the hotel providing a plausible reason. I saw this event as a sign that something bad was going to happen because when one problem starts, it seems like other problems follow alongside. At least that was my experience and belief.

Once again at the hotel, we went to the room where we had met with the dealers. After a short explanation and deliberation, the decision was made to remove everything from me and to pack everything on my husband's body. After this whole exercise, we went back to the taxi, and headed again to the airport. We managed to get through the controls at the Curaçao Airport, lined up in the row at the gate, boarded the plane and finally headed towards Europe with an intercontinental flight.

We landed at the Schiphol Airport in Amsterdam and as soon as the doors opened and the passengers started to leave the airplane, big dogs were walking around them in the tunnel that led to the arrival hall. The dogs were accompanied by some policemen. We were not aware of this development till the moment that we were standing in the line that was moving slowly through the gate corridor. We too had to pass by the dogs and as soon as one of the dogs caught the smell of my husband, he started to jump on his chest and the police requested my husband to stop walking and to step aside towards the wall of the corridor.

The two policemen came towards my husband, put him against the wall and handcuffed him. I stood there at his side, with the baby in my arms and not knowing what to say. One of the officers asked me if I was together with him. It was merely a question for confirmation as we were walking side by side when the dog jumped on Gilly. Upon my affirmative answer, the officer requested me to follow him in the same direction that the other officers had taken Gilly. The police brought me to a questioning room, and my husband was in another room where they were removing all the cocaine from his body. The police started to question me by asking me if I knew that my husband had drugs on him. I lied by saying that I didn't know that until the moment that the dogs jumped on him. I began to deny it and I was crying and saying *"How could he do this to me!"* The officer asked me what happened in Curaçao upon which I explained that we went on a second honeymoon as a celebration of our 7th anniversary. I continued with the statement that I had no reason to believe that my husband would do such thing. The next question was: *"Did you not sense anything in the plane?"*

I replied with: *"My baby was crying since we boarded the plane so I had no time for my husband."* The man looked for a short while at me and told me that I could go.

I took my baby in my arms, walked out of the room and headed towards the baggage claim but in the meanwhile I was thinking of what I would tell my children when I reach home. How will I take care of them, all six of them and have them go to school? I was so confused. I left The Netherlands feeling like we were in a frying pan. Now that we were back, we were in the fire itself!

# CHAPTER FOUR

# POWERS ON THE EARTH

S oon the time would come that I would start experiencing, or better said become aware, of the difference between the power of goodness and the power of evil but before this could happen, I went through a couple of extreme events; with an emphasis on the extreme character of the events.

### *Another downfall*

With Gilly arrested and waiting further developments in his case, I was left alone in charge of our household. The situation at our house was very bad, it went gradually with a fast pace from bad to worse. I didn't know what to do because my husband used to do everything, including the household arrangements. As I explained at the beginning of the book, in my childhood I was not educated and formed in the proper way by my parents and when I grew up, I did not learn the basics on how to conduct a household in a proper way either. I lived for a while at my own place but back then I was only a person with needs. I had the baby, but babies do not complain or act as grown up kids do. My actions including my non-actions at that time were determined by my own needs. Now I had a house full of children to take care of. Each of them with their own desires and needs making the sequence in which actions must be taken very important, but I had no idea what the right sequence should be. I had no idea because I had not practiced; not in my childhood, nor in my pre adulthood and certainly not in my marriage. I was so frustrated with no hope for the future and I thought that I had no other option than to go for a trip. A trip that would help me earn money, enough money to solve my problems.

Despite the last experience at the airport and what Gilly was going through, I decided that I would make another trip. Once again I left the children alone in the house. The baby also stayed in The Netherlands. He stayed with my grandma for a few days. I went back to Curaçao. This time I went with my sister Mariska and we went with the idea that we would carry enough cocaine that would give each of us at least £10.000 (ten thousands British Pound).

We arrived at Curaçao, stayed in the hotel for two weeks and at the end of this period, somebody came and gave to each of us three bottles with the label of a well-known brand of baby powder. He also brought us lots of other baby items like clothing, soap, oil and pampers which were meant as a camouflage for the cocaine. The powders in the vessels were not pure cocaine and we complained that this is not what we had gone to Curaçao for. We expected pure cocaine which would add up more money. Despite the disappointment, we packed the materials provided in our suitcases, left the hotel and headed to the airport in order to catch our flight to Amsterdam. Upon arrival at the airport, we went to the check-in counter, performed all procedures and some minutes later we passed through all the entry and checking points. We boarded the plane and when all passengers were on board, the doors were closed. The plane even started taxing down the runway, but all of a sudden the pilot stopped the plane. We were sitting in the economy class. If I recall well, we were between row 20 and row 30. We looked outside the window searching for the reason why the plane stopped.

> *"Please come with us, you are both suspects".*

We noted that some cars on the runway were heading towards the plane. The cars stopped and some men stepped out. We noticed that one door of the plane was opened because one of the cars with the stairs was put in place. After a short while, we saw four men wearing black coats and holding a pass in their hands walking towards the back of the plane. They stopped like 2 rows before us and one of them asked loudly, *"Please, who are Bianca Morrison and Mariska Grootfaam?"* We looked at each other and without speaking a word; we slowly rose up our hands. The men walked towards us, showed us their passes and said to us: *"Please come with us, you are both suspects".* That is all what the spokesperson of the group said to us. We had no other option so we followed the officers and we walked out of the plane by walking down the removable stairs. Once outside of the plane, we noted that the media was present and the photographers were taking pictures of us. The incident became big news. It was the next day on the front page of the local newspapers and most probably in the headline news on the television of the same evening but I am not sure of the latter one as I had no opportunity to watch the news that night.

After all this media interruption, we were brought to the questioning room at the airport facility. Our suitcases, that were removed from the plane, were there awaiting us. The officers asked us to open the suitcases and to take out the items and display them on the bench and the table that were in front of us. My sister and I did as was requested and we moved every item, one by one. One officer in particular, wearing rubber plastic gloves, took a quick but intense look at the items and then reached for the baby power. He opened it and in the process of opening the vessel, he told us that he was going to slide a stick inside the vessel. He continued saying: *"If the color of the stick changes and turns into purple, we will arrest you"*. He said some more words but I do not remember those anymore. After hearing and processing the information that was provided to us, my sister and I were holding in our breath in anticipation of the outcome of the test. As we were guessing, we left the room handcuffed. Needless to say, we were arrested.

What do you do in such situations? I could not go anywhere. I had plenty of time to think. That was all I could do, think. Still, it was a superficial way of thinking. What would be of my children? My husband was still in jail in The Netherlands and I was arrested on Curaçao. If they sentence me, it could take years before I would be back in The Netherlands. How long will the sentence be? What am I going to do? What can I say? Thoughts and more thoughts.

Through the Dutch Embassy the information that I was arrested reached my family. I was later on informed that my grandmother took the decision to take care of my youngest. The burden would be too heavy for her to take care of the older ones too. The older ones had not much choice. The children's protection bureau was informed of the situation at our house by the Embassy. They went to the house and the children had to go with them to an alternative location. Later on the children were placed in foster homes and institutions.

### God exists!

The officers took us, after we were officially arrested, to police cells that were very close to the airport because we made just a short ride in the car. It was very scary because the lights were off meaning that there was no electricity or at least not in the cells. Nevertheless, the policemen pushed us into the cells. My sister cried from the moment we got arrested and throughout the whole night. Finally, a new day was dawning and the daylight entered the cell slowly but steadily. We stayed for a few days at the location and went through the light-dark-light scenario a couple of times. Ultimately, the policemen brought us to the main prison which is located at the other side of the island. It was a relatively small prison with place for 63 female inmates. When you read chapter 7, you will understand why I say a relatively small prison. The guards on duty gave us towel, toilet paper and soap at the intake point and after that we entered the closed section of the facility. We saw people, factually the inmates, smoking, eating, playing games or doing their own thing but we didn't have anything. The guard showed us our cell and upon entrance we noted that the setup was for four people in one cell with a toilet and shower attached to it. We felt so sad and I told my sister *"Let us talk to God"*. We went down on our knees and prayed: *"God, help us. We are scared and we don't have anything. God, help us! We are scared and we don't have anything. Amen"*. We stood up and walked again around the block and as we saw the same thing as initially, we went back to the cell and to our surprise we found two big bags with provisions awaiting for us. I looked at my sister. She looked at me and said: *"God exists"*.

Church representatives used to come to the prison and hold prayer sessions, counseling sessions and church services for and with the inmates. I used to go, listen and although I didn't really understand what they were saying, I could feel it. The church representative came for Christmas, accompanied by more visitors and they even brought a live band.

When I was in The Netherlands I used to attend a Pentecostal Church and for a while I was in their choir. This was at the time that my oldest children were young and we all went together to the services. At some point I stopped attending the services. Why? I will explain it to you. The daughter of the Pastor of the congregation was the owner of a beauty salon and one day she gave me a hair makeover. As I did not have the money with me at that moment, I promised her that I would pay her later. Soon thereafter a feeling of shame came over me and I felt as if I could not show my face anymore at the services because I had not paid for the hair makeover. Thinking back about the reason why I stopped attending the Church, it is now clear to me that it was an act of the enemy, a deceiving act.

It was at the Pentecostal Church where I learned the songs 'Purify my heart' and 'Jesus loves me' as they were interpreted by Whitney Houston. At the event at the prison at Curaçao, I sang those two songs and everybody was wiping off their tears when I finished. The days went by filled with little to no activity, at least not the ones I was used to. It did not take long for us to be sentenced, and we were sentenced for 18 months. In Curaçao the judge sentences you according to the amount of drugs that you carried.

I used to smoke and even in prison I did so. One day some of the girls and I were smoking hashish and because I was very high on that moment, I went on lying on the lap of Shirley, one of the girls I grouped with in the prison. I was telling her that I wanted to go home, yet knowing that I still had a long time to go till the completion of my sentence. I had just finished my sentence when I heard an officer calling Dinona's name. This girl Dinona had more drugs on her then my sister and I had together and therefore she received a much longer sentence in accordance with the rules applied by the justice system on the island. I laid down when I heard the officer call for Dinona and I was shocked. I asked Shirley, still down on her lap, *"How could they be releasing Dinona before me? She was arrested after me and now she is going before me."* Shirley just laughed. I was pissed off and Shirley kept on laughing. Five minutes later, I heard the officer calling: *"Mariska Grootfaam"*. I said to Shirley: *"What is going on?"* but I couldn't get up because I had smoked too much earlier that day. Shirley did not answer me and just kept on smiling. I thought to myself probably because my sister was crying too much, the authorities decided that she should go. That was the only explanation that I was able to come up with at that moment. I had just finished my quick reasoning when I heard the officer calling: *"Bianca Morrison".* I looked up at Shirley. She was still laughing and said: *"Won't you get up?"* I was stumped and could not answer her. Then, the officer came in and said to me: *"Are you deaf?"* I stood up immediately. The officer continued on saying: *"Amnesia must have affected you".* I was so surprised that I did not react on that. I walked towards the cell to pick up my stuff and together with my sister, I left the prison premises. That was a miracle upon all my sins because I had served only 3 months.

I do not recall well how it all happened after we left the prison premises but finally we arrived in The Netherlands and went on our way to home where another surprise was awaiting for me. The house was empty. The children were not there because they had been taken by the children's' protection bureau and sent to foster homes. My husband was still in prison. My car was sold in order to pay for the bills regarding house rent that was due. I was so frustrated. I thought my life was okay although deep down I knew it was not.

### Neglected God and got arrested again

Once in The Netherlands, I forgot about how good God had been to me while I was imprisoned on Curaçao. Without a means of income and despite the latest experiences, I decided to make a trip again. I lost everything I needed and this was the only way I knew that could help me recover my social status. So I contacted some of my acquaintances and based on the information received, I went on working for Bob, an African native living in The Netherlands. This time I went to Peru, South America. The contacts of my employer picked me up at the airport and took care of me. There in Peru, instead of enhancing my body on the outside with the cocaine, I swallowed it. Nonetheless I got arrested again and this time the sentence was not for eighteen months but for eighty months; six years and eight months.

The prisons in South America are not to be compared with those in Europe where there are minimum human standards to attain to. In South America it is common that families take care of a member that is imprisoned because they know that the standards of living inside those facilities are very low. The prison in Peru had a marketplace where the inmates could buy what they want. The marketplace offered everything you could imagine. There was even a beauty salon. To buy stuff on the marketplace and/or for additional services meant that you should have financial means. My family did not really care for me during the time that I was in prison in Peru. My dad was the only one who cared but could not do much. I was in contact with the Dutch Embassy through an officer that would come every 3 months and provide me with an allowance in the amount of EUR 30 which was provided as a courtesy of a Dutch Foundation to all Dutch citizen imprisoned abroad.

Throughout the years I had developed a theft and reckless spending habit and as a result I did not know how to handle money therefore, while being in the prison, I was always in debt. In order to make use of services in the prison, I was always crediting items till the moment would come that the money from the Embassy arrived. Now I know that God was trying to teach me during those days, how life is but I didn't understand. It took me long time but I understood that when you don't have the Spirit of God, you have no direction in your life. I had accepted the aforementioned for real but this happened in my life not when I was in Peru, but a long time after that.

Soon after the police had arrested me at the airport of Peru, I was sent to the Santa Monica Female prison which is located in the capital city Lima. This prison is where females, locals and foreigners, who were arrested for drugs matters, are sent. Although the day to day conditions were not the best, there were activities and moments that had brightened the days of the inmates or at least, mine got enlightened. One of these moments was the visits of the church representatives. This prison received visits of representatives of the Roman Catholic, Presbyterian, Pentecost, and Jehovah Witness and there were even some missionaries from Canada who came two times a week for fellowship with the English speaking inmates. The representatives of the churches were in general locals, speaking Spanish and they refused to speak English so I was forced to learn the local language. In this prison I learnt how to pray and fast.

Furthermore, around October 2003, I joined a prayer group with the Pentecostals and I also started to recite the rosary with the Roman Catholics. I kept on praying with the teams till my last moments in the prison. I have to admit that in that period of my life, I was so ignorant regarding the prayers and the power that they have and I believe this is because I was always praying in Spanish. I didn't realize that it was for real and the lack of this notion let to the fact that I would throw away all of this right after my release from prison.

After the initial period with the prayer teams, time had passed and spring would soon begin. Spring meant in this prison the arrival of a major event. The prison management organized, or allowed for the organization of, a beauty pageant among the inmates and this pageant was called Miss Prima Vera which means Miss Spring. I was informed upfront that this was always a big happening and indeed I experienced it as was described to me. A casting organization used to come every year to the prison and they would look for the most beautiful ladies in the prison. The lady who wins, would get a contract as a professional model for TV and magazines, an amount of money and also several beauty products. After experiencing all of this, it became my wish that when I came out of prison, to have a program to promote prisoners with talents. My talent, which is singing, did not remain undiscovered. For this competition I would sing every year during the show. Several TV stations and other media covered the show and it had not taken long before I appeared on the front page of the newspapers with the header 'The singing angel in prison'. My appearance in the newspaper with a positive note had not happen once but surprisingly three times, in 2003, 2004 and 2005. In 2005 one of the TV stations even made a documentary about me which led to the fact that even the president came to the prison facilities in order to meet and see me in person. The unexpected visit of the president had a positive outcome for me that I had not dreamed of. After his visit I had received grace and I was released earlier.

*Picture of a performance at the Santa Monica
that appeared in a newspaper in Peru.*

*Old habits and their consequences*

My moments of fame in Peru had provided me an earlier release from prison and also the chance to sing in the country but immediately as I got out of prison I forgot about God which made it easier to fall back into my old habits. I started with my old life again partially because I had some arrangements made with an inmate who had become my friend whose serving time would end soon after my early release. Her name was Rachel and she was originally from Nigeria. While we were in prison she had introduced me to a Peruvian lady called Juana who was the owner of a big hotel in Lima. Juana stood bail for me so that I could make use of the opportunity of early release from prison and she offered me accommodation at her hotel.

The hotel was in the district called Lurigancho which by car lies approximately 30 minutes away from the center of Lima. I went to Juana's hotel, stayed there for two months waiting for Rachel to come out of prison and in the mean time that I was waiting for Rachel, I had some fun. I was back to my old habits and I had forgotten about the Lord.

When I was in prison, I used to write to a guy named Eves and he on his turn used to send me letters in the weekends with money and flowers. He was very romantic. He was also from Suriname but lived in French Guyana. I called him every day in the move because he got out of prison around the same time that I was released. The two of us met regularly, we had a lot of fun including sex, but within a short period he got sick. It is because of this situation that I can really say that God really loves me and protects me. Eves had fever so I asked him: *"What is wrong with you?"*

He said to me: "*I have gonorrhea*". Gonorrhea is a sexually trans-mitted disease (STD) that can infect men and women. It is a very common infection and it can cause infections in the genitals, rectum, and throat. This disease can be treated and cured with the right medication.[1] I continued asking him: "*How can you get that after being for such a long time in prison?*" upon which he answered: "*If you have money, they allow you to have sex with prostitutes*". I became so scared because I had slept with him and I had no guarantee that I had not been infected by him. I informed Juana of the situation and she bought some medicine for Eves which had helped him getting better. On my turn, I went to the doctor but luckily, nothing happened to me and I thank God for that. This situation really scared me and made me put one part of my old habits on hold. From that point onwards, the other part took it all.

---

[1] Gonorrhea - CDC Fact Sheet retrieved from http://www.cdc.gov/std/gonorrhea/stdfact-gonorrhea.htm on July 2, 2015

*Bianca and two other inmates*
*at the prison in Peru*

# CHAPTER FIVE

# BETRAYAL, CORRUPTION AND MORE

M y friend Rachel came out of prison around the expected time and we were so glad to meet again in the liberty of the free world. We went to a club to celebrate and we met some Nigerian friends, who used to come to Juana's hotel as well. They were very friendly. I got the opportunity in Peru to perform on stage for the same people who used to come to the Santa Monica Female Prison. I did that for like two months, but then I ended the working relationship, because Rachel made it clear that she wanted to go back to her daughter in Spain. We then worked on ways to get out of Peru.

### Getting out of Peru

Travelling on the usual way and on a short notice became a problem as I had no passport and neither did Rachel. My passport was still at the courthouse and in order to get it back, I would have to sign some papers and stay in the country for the period as determined by the authorities. The main issue was that the last time when I went to the courthouse and asked for my passport, it felt like they wanted to re-open my case. With that in mind, I had no wish to stay any longer in Peru. Rachel said to me, after we became aware of the complications around our paperwork: *"We have to leave the country."* The question was then how. We informed Juana what was going on and she told us to be ready at three o'clock the next morning because we would have to sneak out and take a taxi to the bus station. We did as was explained to us and when we arrived at the bus station, Juana bought tickets for the three of us and we walked to the bus that was travelling to a city close to the border with Ecuador.

We decided that Rachel and I would not sit next to each other in the bus in case that a control would be conducted by authorities. Should there be a control and asked for our passports, we would be able to explain our story as two persons that do not know each other. We traveled for like 16 hours and during all that time we had talked to nobody; not even to each other. It was very scary but thanks to God, there was no passport control. Around midnight we arrived at the border of Ecuador which was also the last stop of the bus line we were on. Everybody stepped out of the bus. Juana wished us all the best, we hugged her and then she took the next bus back to Lima. Rachel and I stood at the bus station and watched the bus of Juana disappear in the darkness of the night.

There at the bus station we had to decide what to do next. The only option we actually had was to get into a taxi, but I told Rachel that if the driver is going to cross the border, the border patrol will surely ask for our passports. She got scared and I was also scared, but somebody had to be bold, so we stepped into a taxi and I told the taxi driver the truth. I told him that we were on the run. He said to my surprise: *"No problem. Give me 100 dollar each and I will get you across the border."* We agreed that the fee was fine and we proceeded. The driver took me along, while Rachel was waiting in the car. He held me at my waist like I was his girlfriend which I didn't like at all, but what could I do? He was not attractive at all. He told me that we would pass where the soldiers are so I should keep quiet. My heart was beating very fast. The moment he saw the soldiers, he kissed me on my mouth. It was so horrible, but it helped. The soldiers were laughing and one of them made the comment: *"Hey, brother! Is all of that for you alone?"* He smiled, but didn't talk and we passed the border. The same way he managed to get Rachel over the border. After this comedy, the driver went to get the car, picked us up on Ecuador territory and drove us to the nearest hotel.

> *"No problem. Give me 100 dollar each and I will get you across the border."*

We were so happy that we had arrived at the hotel without having any problem, but then the driver came with his last surprise act by telling us that he wanted to sleep with both of us. I told him that his last request was absolutely not part of the agreement we made earlier. He didn't force us, but you could see on his face and from his actions that he was disappointed. Immediately after he left, I told Rachel that we should leave the place because as we didn't sleep with the driver, he might inform the immigration about us on his way back to Peru. We left the hotel without hesitating and searched for another one.

We crossed a couple of streets and around three o'clock in the morning we entered another hotel. When we settled in the room, Rachel went on to call a brother who was living in Spain. He told her, that we were still too close to the border. Therefore he would send a friend to pick us up in one hour time and to bring us to the next city. The friend, a lady, came. We entered her car and took seat in the back. We were driving on a road what was totally dark with only bush around it. Seriously, if you don't have a strong heart, you would not make it. I can tell you that!

The lady told us once we were getting near the city we were heading to, that we should not talk for a while because the people could hear that we were foreigners. She had barely finished her sentence when we heard someone shout in Spanish language *"Stop your car"*. My heart started pumping very quickly and Rachel grabbed my hand. Her hand was cold and sweaty. The lady driver reacted very cool. She stayed calm and asked *"Who is the overall boss?"* We noted that as an answer to her question, one person stepped forward. She showed him some papers and as she was doing that, she put some money in his hands. Immediately all the guns and rifles were lifted up. The driver finalized the conversation with the leader of the rebels and continued driving. Once we left the unofficial check point, our rescuer looked at us through the back mirror and said: *"You can relax. We passed"*.

At that moment I exhaled and I realized that I had been holding my breath in. It turned out that the lady was the wife of a soldier. She brought us to the barracks which they and some soldiers were using as their living space.

## New adventures on the way

After we stayed for one month in the barracks, we still didn't have a passport while our rescuer was collecting money from the guy who was living in Spain based on the promise that she would get passports for us. It was all a lie. After those 30 days, Rachel had reached a point that she would not wait anymore and she was determined to leave even if she had to do it without me. I had no intention to stay there on my own, so we left the barracks without informing the lady, our presumed rescuer. We took the public transportation towards the city of Guayaquil where we went to a hotel. Soon after we installed ourselves in the hotel, Rachel went to the Embassy of Spain. Because she had her ID with her, she was able to prove who she was which made it possible for her to get a passport. This move of Rachel was absolutely necessary as the guy in Spain was getting tired of sending us money.

There was still one problem. I didn't have anything with me to identify myself. Rachel was the one spending money on me and soon she said that I had to make an effort to find a solution to my problem. If not, she would leave me there. She gave me 100 dollars for me to call my family in order to come up with a solution. I called my ex-husband Gilly and I told him of my problem. At that time he was already my ex-husband because when he got out of prison, I was imprisoned in Peru, and he had filed for divorce.

Fortunately, Gilly had accepted my call and he took the time to look into my stuff that was still in the house. He told me on phone: *"you have a passport here but it just expired last month"*. I used to change my passport very often because of the business I was in. Gilly promised me that he would send the passport to me and the next day I received it at the hotel from the transporter of DHL. I was very happy but the problem was not over, only partially solved. I still had to go to the Embassy for them to provide me with a valid passport. I went to the Dutch Embassy in Guayaquil and I lied when the officer asked me where my other, or better said the valid, passport was. I told the story that I was not living with my husband anymore because he was always beating me up and I was afraid to go to the house to get my valid papers. The officer told me that before they could issue a new passport for me, they would perform some investigation and I should go and come back the next day. I showed up the next day and they gave me a new passport. Through some contacts of the guy in Spain we got information on how to obtain stamps for our passports to prove that we had entered Ecuador on a legal way. Rachel and I went to the address that was given to us. We met the lawyer, who was a friend of a friend. He gave us the required stamps, the out-stamp for Peru and the in-stamp for Ecuador in our passports. Each of us had to pay 200 dollar for the illegal stamps. After this action, we were ready for the next step.

### Moving to the other side of South America

As soon as we both had a valid passport, we bought tickets to Venezuela which is also in South America and is a neighbor of Suriname. We had planned to go to Suriname to collect cocaine for transportation as this was the main reason why the guy in Spain had been taking care of us by sending money. We took public transportation and reached the international airport of Guayaquil, the second largest airport in Ecuador. We were still afraid, because we were not sure that the in and out stamps visible in our passports, were real because we got them from the underground circuit. Thanks to God, we passed all the controls without any complication and in the plane we cried because we succeeded. We were happy and not aware that more problems were just around the corner. Once we reached the Venezuelan airport, we ran out of money. Rachel called her 'brother' again; he simply said that he won't send us money until we had reached Suriname. Rachel got upset and she told me that I had to try something now, because she had already tried, but in vain. I went to the immigration and told the officer that we were on transit but a pickpocket had stolen my wallet. We still had to buy tickets to Suriname. However the unexpected event created the need for me to contact my family and request them to send money over. I asked the officer if we could please enter the country for just a few days so I could call my family to send the money. The man agreed as he felt pity for us and he even brought us to a hotel. He liked Rachel a lot so he came at night and picked her up for a date.

In the meantime I called my dad and I told him *"Dad, I have been released from prison and I don't have money"*. He told me that he was expecting my phone call because I only looked for him when I was in need. That remark made me feel guilty. That is why I said to him that when I was back in The Netherlands, I would work on building a new relationship with him. He continued telling me: *"Don't worry. In 15 minutes time somebody will meet you at the hotel"*.

When I finished my call, Rachel had come back to the room, and I told her what I had discussed. She didn't believe me however, we went together to the lobby of the hotel to wait for the visitor my dad had told me about and, behold, a big grey jeep stopped in front of the hotel, and a bold headed guy stepped out of the car into the lobby. The man looked around in the lobby and then asked: *"Who is Bianca?"* Rachel and I were standing at the entrance of the lobby, so we heard him. I answered: *"I am Bianca"*. He replied to me: *"Your dad asked me to come and seek you."* I said then: *"Okay, follow me to my room."* The three of us went to the elevators and from there to the room. I opened the door for us to enter the room. The visitor went on to sit down on the carpet and proceeded by deepening his hand into his pocket, took out 3000 dollars and gave them to me. I was so happy that my father had answered my call for help. Rachel and I did not waste time. We packed our bags, or the little that we had carried with us, we checked out of the hotel and the visitor drove us to the airport where we went to a travel agent counter and we bought tickets for that same night to Trinidad.

We were still on our way to Suriname with the aim to traffic cocaine however in order to enter Suriname, I needed a Surinamese visa. Though my parents were born in Suriname, the fact that I was born in The Netherlands was the reason why I needed a visa. I wanted to transit in Trinidad in order to enter the country and get the required visa there. I would soon learn that some choices are better to not be made.

*From one trouble into another*

The ride to the airport, the purchasing of a plane ticket and boarding of the plane to Trinidad went well. So far so good. I had everything worked out in my mind. From the moment we would land at the Trinidad airport till the moment I would have the visa in my hand. With this plan in mind, we stepped out of the flight and we walked as usual to the passport control to stand in the line. Rachel stood in the line besides me. At my turn, I gave my passport and ticket to the gentlemen and as he was checking the documents, I asked him, *"Please sir, can you please tell me where I can find a Suriname Embassy here?"* The man did not answer me. He kept looking at my ticket, and finally he asked me to go and sit down on the bench nearby. So I did and I noticed that also Rachel was sent to sit down and wait. We sat next to each other and I asked her: *"What is going on? Why are they delaying us? Or are they thinking that we have drugs with us?"*

Suddenly a female officer came and she said to us, *"Please follow me"*. There was no smile on her face. The officer brought us to a cell and locked us up without providing any explanation. We stayed there till the next morning. Another female officer came to us around six in the morning, she opened the cell and some other female officers entered in order to check all our stuff including a body search. Later in the afternoon they came to a conclusion since they didn't find anything. I took the opportunity to ask to them: *"Please, may I know what is going on? And why we are treated like this?"* Then one of the officers answered: *"Please madam Morrison, you came with a one way ticket. Don't you know that it is forbidden?"*

I said: *"Excuse me. I came here just as a transit passenger to get my visa for Suriname so why should I buy a retour ticket?"* The officer then told me: *"Sorry madam, it is against the law so we will send you back to Venezuela"*. Then they proceeded by asking me: *"Do you have money with you?"* We had 2,000 dollars left for our tickets to Suriname. They took it from us including our tickets and gave us a bail out of 500 dollars. Rachel was so pissed off that she said that if she would had known all of this beforehand, she would have left me in Ecuador because only bad luck had followed us on the way.

There we were again on a flight but not to Suriname as planned but to the neighbor. When we reached Venezuela, the passengers and airport personnel saw us with handcuffs on. The officials took us to their office and questioned and searched us, because they couldn't understand what was going on. First we told them that pickpocket had stolen our money, and therefore they had allowed us to enter the country. We managed to fly to Trinidad, but the authorities there had sent us back. It was so suspicious but fortunately they could not find anything so they had to allow us to enter the country again. This time I did not call my dad, but I called the guy who had helped us out the other day directly and he came faithfully. I explained to him what had happened and he did not make a problem of it and gave us some money again. When we finally had the money, I was so glad. Rachel was ready to leave me behind but then again she said to me: *"I won't fly unless you find a Suriname Embassy here in Venezuela"*.

I looked quickly through the phone book in the hotel room, and yes, I found one. I don't know why I had not thought of that earlier. All the same, we took a taxi and went to the address that I had written down from the phone book. When we arrived and I saw the Suriname flag, a joyful feeling caught hold of me. We entered the building and a nice lady welcomed us. She told us to fill in a form. Each of us had to deposit 50 dollars and then she said that we should come back after 3 days. Rachel did not like that idea, but what else could we do? After 3 days we went back to the Embassy and everything was fine. The officer stamped the passports and we went straight to the airport and bought a ticket to Aruba and from Aruba to Suriname.

> **.... and all the passports were lost.**

*It was not over yet*

After all the adventures, the plane we were in finally landed at the Suriname airport. We walked to the passport control where another surprise was waiting for us. We handed over our documents to the officer for the passport control and we got the reaction from the officer that he would confiscate our passports because we travelled with a one way ticket. He proceeded by telling us that because my parents were from there he would let us enter the country, but we had to buy tickets back to The Netherlands and then we could come to pick up our passport at the military office. We had no choice other than to do as we were instructed, but first we had some other issues to handle.

We left the airport facilities and went on to stay for two days with pa Eddy, the fetish priest that I had mentioned before. He gladly welcomed us at his house. The next day Rachel and I went to the international phone house to call Rachel's friend in Spain. He was so glad that we had finally arrived in Suriname and therefore he sent us money through a money transfer company. We drove to the office of the money transfer company to cash out the money and after that we proceeded to pay both our plain tickets to The Netherlands as was instructed and finally we went to the Military head office. Once we had reached there, we met the same gentleman who had confiscated our passports at the airport. We showed him the tickets and he came with an explanation that they had renovated the building and all the passports were lost. Rachel got so annoyed, because she had already said in the past that I was bad luck to her. The new problem was that Spain had no Embassy in Suriname and the Dutch Embassy could not understand why I wanted a passport if I just had gotten a new one four days before. Then again, I had no ID card to prove who I was. I was so stressed. On the other hand, the Dutch Embassy gave Rachel the address of a Spanish lady who was supposed to be the Spanish Consulate. We went there and after three weeks Rachel got her new passport. At that time I had nothing yet because the Embassy was investigating my case. Our stay in Suriname took a long curve, much longer than we had wanted.

### They betrayed me

Due to the latest developments, I had introduced Rachel to my friend named Daisy who helped us by permitting us to stay in one of her houses. She was a very close friend of mine and earlier in my story, I had spoken about her. We used to go to her place and have a nice chat, but soon after she was talking a lot alone with Rachel, and started acting strange towards me.

She had never shown this kind of behavior towards me before. I started wondering why this change till one day I saw a lady, who I did not know, together with Daisy and Rachel. They were sitting in the garden and they were fixing on hair weave, synthetic hair. It was not normal weave because this one was filled with cocaine. Rachel told me that she couldn't wait longer for me and that she was going back to Spain. They went on finishing the fitting of the hair and after that Daisy and the lady brought Rachel and me back to the house where we were staying. There Rachel swallowed like a pallet of cocaine. While she was swallowing the drugs, I was cleaning the house. Around six o'clock in the evening Daisy picked her up, and brought her to the airport. I was left alone in the house and all I was thinking of, was what would happen to me next.

Daisy came back around Midnight and told me that I had to leave the house. She gave me no explanation. She, of all people, told me to leave. After all that Daisy and I had been through in the past and despite a friendship of over three years, she put me aside. After all that Rachel and I had experienced in these last 9 months, she also put me aside. Both of them betrayed me.

All I could do at that moment was, to look for ways to keep on surviving. Nothing more and nothing less.

# CHAPTER SIX

# GOING BACK AND FORTH

B efore continuing with the story, I want you to take the time to say the following prayer. If possible say out loud.

*Father in heaven, what I will read in the upcoming chapters is for my understanding on how evil forces operate, moreover for me to understand how compassionate and pure Your love is that You do not withstand those that had been on the wrong path that seek for You once they realize that they were on the wrong path.*
*Father, protect me from all forces sent by the enemy of our souls to steal, kill and destroy. Father, cover me and surround me with the precious blood of Jesus, send Your angels to fight for me in the spiritual realms and the Holy Spirit to guide me. Amen.*

## Old habits revived

I was in Suriname when I got the cold shower from Daisy and Rachel. Luckily, I was in a country and a city where I had been before. About 5 years had gone by since my last visit which meant that circumstances, infrastructure and social atmosphere had changed. Nonetheless there was still a lot that was familiar to me and Daisy was not the only person that I knew. There were more people who had known me in my time of abundance and well-being and I did not want for them to become aware of my current state. For that reason, I disregarded going to the house of my families in Suriname or to the house I still owned. If I went to those locations, it would reflect on a very short timeframe that I was not able to provide for my own day-to-day needs like food. I knew that an old friend of mine, who also lived abroad, was in town and I decided to go to her place to see if she would help me out.

I arrived at the place with the intention to explain immediately what had happen to me but to my surprise, she met me in front of the house and told me to take a seat and wait for her; she would be back in a minute. I did as requested though a feeling of sadness came upon me. I sat on the balcony, in front of the house, when all of a sudden, a car stopped on the road, just in front of the house. The person that stepped out of the car was Rick, the brother of my friend. He saw me sitting on the balcony, walked towards me and hugged me. We had not seen each other for years. He said: *"How are you?"* That question triggered me and before I finalized my thoughts on what to answer, the words had rolled out of my mouth. I told him what happened in the last 6 months. He told me not to worry. He invited me to step into his car and he took me to his village. He took good care of me for the time that I had stayed there.

Furthermore he helped me with the procedures in order to obtain a new passport. After three months I got my passport and I was able to travel back to The Netherlands. I had my passport, a ticket but no money of my own. In order to receive money for my expenses once I arrive in The Netherlands, I swallowed one kilo of cocaine. I can surely say that the friends that I had in that season of my life, had one thing in common which is expecting, at minimum, a fair return for everything they do for you. All the help that I had received during my last months in Suriname, was partially for the sake of the good friendship and partially it served as pre-work phase, because the drug I brought to The Netherlands was for Rick.

### Rejoining my sister, my children and my passion

I left Suriname with Rick. We encountered no problems when leaving Suriname or entering The Netherlands. My sister Mariska, who was happy to see me after such a long time, picked us up from the airport. Rick went home with us because the two of us had one transaction pending. My sister did not know that I had cocaine with me, so when we reached her house, I couldn't hold it anymore and I had to confess the situation to her. She didn't like it, but what could she had done at that moment? After the confession, I went to the bathroom and toilet that was combined in one room and I extracted all of the cocaine out of my body. Once finished, I gave the product to Rick. He gave me £15,000 (approximately €22,000) in return, took a cab and went further on his own way. I felt like I was the queen with all that money and I used it without thinking that one day I could ran out of money.

I stayed with my sister and I also used to sleep at my grandmother's place. I did not want to move in at my ex-husbands place for the reason that he wanted me to change, and despite all I had been through, I had not reached that point yet. Because of my own behavior our paths remained separated. My ex-husband was a good father that had taken care of his children as soon as he had gotten out of prison. Once he had a fixed place for living and a fixed form of income, this time a legal income, he did all that was possible to get the custody of the children. At last, he received permission for the children to stay with him every weekend and during vacations. God bless him for his efforts and dedication towards the children.

Once I was settled again in The Netherlands, I got in touch with my children. The first time I had seen them again, was an emotional encounter. They had grown and I was happy that all of them were healthy. As I was staying at my sister's place there was no space for them to move in with me permanently. The only alternative was weekend stayover. They used to come over regularly. After some weeks I noticed that my sister started acting strange but she did not say anything. The next weekend, my children came over just as the weeks before. However, this time something had changed. Immediately after their departure on Sunday evening, my sister started complaining that my children were eating all of her food and that she could no longer tolerate it. I ran out of money, what I had earned with my last drug transport, and since my return in The Netherlands, I had not worked at least not on things that had brought up enough money.

After I had moved in with my sister, there were two things I had worked on which were singing and making efforts to increase the self-esteem of other people. There was a famous music group in the mid 2000's called Wolf Pack featuring Ill Kid and some other members. I had joined the group after being introduced to them by my sister. My sister had introduced me to the group because she wanted me to stop with the drug business and since I loved to sing, she thought that coupling me with the group was the perfect solution. Considering the fact that music and singing were my passion, I did not even doubt when I got the question to think about joining the group. Mariska was my manager. We had given a couple of performances, but the money I had earned with singing was not enough. The other thing I had been working on is something that started more by accident, but with a great human value.

> *"Say, I am a queen, I am a diamond, and I am not depressed."*

One day I was walking in the mall and I felt in my spirit that my sister was sad, so I decided to buy her some items to cheer her up. I bought her a card, a rose and I went to her place. Truly, when I arrived there, she was lying in her bed and she was depressed. I entered the bedroom, sat beside her while holding the items I had bought behind me, and I asked her what was wrong with her. She told me: "*I am fat and ugly*". I took the items from my back, showed them to her and encouraged her to get up, look inside the mirror and tell herself that she is beautiful.

I said to her: "*Say, I am a queen, I am a diamond, and I am not depressed.*" And she did so. The next day I went back to see how she was doing and a happy person opened the door for me. I was so glad to see her in that shape. We went on to sit on chairs in the living room and she picked up her laptop to show me that she had written down all the words that I had told her the other day. She continued by telling me that she wanted to write a book that would encourage other people that could be in the same depressed situation that she had been in.

As a result of this conversation, we started a project for women with a big posture and low self-respect. We started this program because we had big postures ourselves and we knew what it was to have a low self-esteem and the consequences thereof. The book, which my sister was talking about that she wanted to write, became later on a reality. Her book came out in 2012 and it is titled 'Op weg naar je droom' which means 'On the way to your dream'. As I had mentioned before, what I had been doing those days, had not delivered much money which led to my sister's complain.

After my sister's complain about the food, I decided to look for a formal job. After some searching around in the neighborhood and contacting some employment agencies, I got two formal jobs. I worked from nine to five as a telemarketing seller for the agency named Randstad and at night I worked in the post office. At the post office I met a guy named Carmelo. He was very nice to me, and he even helped me with my work. We had to arrange items that had to be sent to destinations all over the world by inserting the area code of the packages in the machines; like you insert information in a laptop. One night we had a break at the same time and we decided to have a meal together. Later on, when we had finished our work, he offered me a ride home and while he was driving the car, I told him who I was and I also told him that I loved singing. He said: *"Oh, this is a coincidence. I'm also a musician."* He continued his story by telling me that he was a member of a famous rap group named 'Official Niggers' featuring Sugar Cane as the leader and coordinator. His artistic (rap) name was M.D. and he gave me a demonstration of his singing talent in the car. I had to admit that he was very good. I let him drive me to my grandmother's house and when we arrived, I invited him in so he could hear a C.D. where I was singing about pain. The C.D. contained material that I had recorded together with the group Wolf Pack. I told Carmelo how come I became a member of the group and I also told him of the weekend stay-overs of my children that were still current. He then asked me: *"Are you sure that the weekend stayovers will not create trouble between you and your sister?"* I assured him that it would not be a problem as the one problem we had, was already solved. My friendship with Carmelo developed into a relationship and I was so in love with Carmelo.

My children were still coming over for the weekends, but I was more and more at Carmelo's place. All went well till one weekend that my kids came to my sister place, and I was not yet there. My sister, who had had enough of the situation, did not want to receive them so they had to return home. On the other hand, Carmelo told me that he was not ready for children, reason for which I could not receive the children at his place. I was so sad about the situation but I had no alternatives.

*Rather by chance than by choice*

Carmelo had introduced me to his mates in the band and because I went with him to the studio often, I got acquainted with the other guys. One day Carmelo told me that he had not paid the rent of his house for already three months and if he would not pay that month, he would have to leave and he did not have an idea how to fulfill the obligations nor did he have an alternative location. This conversation took place not long after the situation at my sister's place. What made the situation more complicated for me was the fact that after the situation at my sister's place, I went to stay more and more at my grandmothers' house. Because I liked to smoke indian hemp, I did not want to stay there any longer just to avoid that my grandmother would have any problem with me for my smoking habit. So in short, I had no place to go where I felt that I could be myself and do what I want. One day after work, I went to the studio and I stayed the whole night in the studio singing and writing my music. I did not want the guys to know that I had no place to stay. This repeated itself for a couple of days.

> *I was in that moment of despair, and troubled by my thoughts, when I heard someone call my name.*

One morning, I left the studio and I just went out walking with no fixed plan. I ended up in a shopping mall in the southeast part of Amsterdam, called 'Amsterdamse Poort'. I was walking around and I was crying. I cried because I had no fixed place where I could stay and it was almost weekend, the time that I had the opportunity to be with my kids. I was in that moment of despair, and troubled by my thoughts, when I heard someone call my name. I looked up and saw that the person, who was calling my name, was the wife of Bob, the man who once had employed me to carry cocaine from Peru to The Netherlands.

The lady said to me: *"My husband is looking for you. Here is the phone. Please talk to him"*. I realized that she must had been talking with Bob, when she saw me and called me. I took the phone from her and I greeted Bob. After a short greeting, he said to me: *"Please come to Ghana. I am in a crisis and I need your help"*. I told him: *"I cannot"* but he kept begging me. Finally, I gave the phone back to the lady and had the intention to walk away when the lady asked me for my phone number. I gave it to her without thinking of the implications and I continued my walk. Bob called me later on by phone and continued with his plead for me to travel to Ghana. The situation I was in at that moment, combined with the wish to be together with my children, made me accept the offer.

I had not accepted right off. After a couple of calls and some extensive thinking, I saw the offer as the perfect solution. Once I had decided to go, I told my daughter Channelta that I was going to Ghana to carry cocaine. I also told her that when I would be back, I would be able to rent a house where they could be together with me. I told all my children the truth. They were all aware of the situation and did not like the idea.

Preparations for my travel were made by Bob. I had planned to stay only four days in Ghana so that my relatives, especially my sister and my ex-husband, would not find out that I had been out of the country. Exactly on the day that I had to travel, I received a phone call from Gilly and another one from my sister Mariska. I saw the incoming calls but I did not pick them up. Gilly had left a message on my voice mail in which he told me that I should pick up Margillio from school. Once I had listened to his message, I called him back and told him that I was travelling to Ghana therefore I could not pick our son up from school. He started asking me why I was travelling that day and he continued telling me that I should come back, that I was a useless mother and so on. He spoke all kinds of insults towards me but I did not mind him. I had not returned the call of Mariska therefore she had no idea where I was or where I was heading to.

I proceeded with my initial plan and travelled to Africa. I arrived at the Kotoka International Airport in Ghana and my first impression of the country was way different from what I had imagined. All I knew of the continent of Africa was from TV programs that showed Africa as a place full of animals and people living in huts. I was expecting to see all of that. It was already late in the evening when the plane landed at the airport. The passengers waited patiently till the moment the pilot said that the doors could be opened. I followed the other passengers to the check points and further to the baggage claim. After all the required checks I managed to reach the baggage claim area, took hold of my baggage and walked to the exit doors for the arrival hall. Once outside I saw Bob. He had called me on the phone and made the proposal for me to go to Ghana. I entered the car where he had been waiting for me and we drove away. To my surprise, Africa was not full of huts and animals but the city was just like home. The city had normal streets, shops and I did not see half naked people walking around, but well-dressed people. We drove through the city till we reached the place where I had to stay for the night. Bob told me that I should go inside by showing me through which door I had to enter and gave some instructions for when I would be inside. He said that he would come back the next day. I entered the building and noticed that the light would not turn on and I got so scared. I couldn't see where I was or what was really in my near surroundings. Therefore I had to find my way to the room that Bob had indicated by walking with one hand along the wall. At last, I found the room. I sat on the bed till the next morning. When it became day and the sunlight entered the room, I took the courage to open the door and look into the hall.

I decided to have a walk inside the house. It was big and beautiful. I realized that I was in a big house which I think had more than eleven rooms. While I was on the tour, I saw a gentleman with two ladies coming down the stairs. I guessed that they had had a good time together last night. The gentleman introduced himself to me and continued by telling the ladies that they should bring me to town so I could buy whatever I would need. He gave me the money and the ladies and I went on shopping. I bought some dresses, had my hair and nails done and went to the supermarket to buy some items so that I could cook the next day. After we returned to the house and unpacked the items bought, I was brought to the gentleman's house where I met his children. They were nice kids and liked me a lot.

## *The decision was not mine*

The four days had gone by fast and the day that I had to travel, arrived quickly. It was almost time to travel when I felt in my spirit that something was not good. I told Bob that I wanted to perform my spiritual bath before I travel and therefore I had to buy some items. We went to the shops where I bought a cock, an egg, a beer, white chalk, a calabash, white candle, a red candle, a clay pot and some other stuff. Then we went to the bush to pick up some leaves and I finalized the shopping round with the purchase of a bottle of white gin so I could prepare the water for my bath. I did exactly, what pa Eddy used to do. He would put newspapers on the floor, and then he would put the leaves on top of it and paint the leaves with white chalk. Then he would put them inside the pot and proceed to arrange the drinking bottles inside, place the egg in the middle, but before placing the egg, he would put some gin in his mouth then blow it three times on the egg. In the meantime he would clean the cock and put it on fire with no salt and no pepper, just like that, because after the bath the person would spread the food on the plantain leaves and eat it. There was a specific way of eating it: you throw one behind your back and then eat a portion. You keep on repeating this sequence till it is finished.

After this, the candles are placed each at one side of the banana leaves. When the person undergoing the process was taking the bath, he/she had to take the egg and hold it in the right hand where the moon is shining and you have to break it. If the egg does not break, that means trouble. I made also a medicine made out of castor oil, cookies, coffee and cigar. You mix all the ingredients together in a pot on the day that you travel and you rub the mixture on your face so that the authorities would not see you. I performed all of the aforementioned procedures.

I did it all but the result was not what I was hoping for. While I was bathing, my egg had not broken and from that moment on I knew that there was trouble. I told Bob that I wanted to do the ritual all over again because if not, the authorities would arrest me. Bob just told me that I was too paranoid and that I should calm down. I started to cry and in order to calm me down he brought me to a pastor. The pastor told me that I would be arrested for a murder case but I would remain only as a suspect. After having heard all of this, I continued on crying. It was a deep and intense cry. Bob who had brought me to the pastor told me that I should not mind the pastor because what he had said was a fake prophecy. He brought me to another pastor, not one in the city but this time one in the bush. There were more people at the location and the pastor called me in the middle and they came and stood around me. The pastor rubbed oil on me and told me that all is fine with me. I kept on crying all the while at the location of the second pastor. I could not stop. Bob brought me to another evangelist, who prayed for me and there I really wept all the tears I had out of me. We went back to the house after this last try.

Once at the house, I told Bob that I really did not want to do it. He told me: *"There is no turning back. You should try to do your best"*. He gave me a plastic bowl with hundred items containing cocaine. I started swallowing them one by one and by the time I had swallowed like fifty, I began to vomit. Consequently, I had to start all over again. While trying for the second time, I said to myself that the fact that I had vomited was a sign that I would be in problem. I forced myself to swallow more than fifty and I realized that I couldn't make it. I called Bob to inform him and he told me that if I couldn't swallow all, they would wrap some in a condom in order for me to insert it in my vagina. The remaining would be put on the exterior of my body. I told him that the last two requests was too much and why couldn't he see or recognize that the signs were too much. He didn't mind at all what I had said. He took the items that I had not swallowed and prepared them for the new transportation method as he had told me. He even helped me to push the last part into my body. After all the merchandise was settled for transportation, we left the house and headed towards the airport for me to catch the plane to Amsterdam.

# CHAPTER SEVEN

# IMPRISONED ONCE MORE

### *Arrested for the third time*

It was May 20th, 2006. The day that according to my plane ticket, I had to fly to Amsterdam. We drove from the location where I had stayed to the Kotoka International Airport; a ride of less than 20 minutes. I stepped out of the car, took my belongings and entered the airport building. Bob just drove away.

I was not even 5 minutes at the airport when I got arrested. I had walked from the main entrance to the line for the check-in counter when some officials called me on the side, and requested: *"Please, can we have your passport?"* I opened my purse, took the passport and gave it to them. Bob had told me that if someone is arrested in Ghana, he/she could pay an amount and the authorities would let that person go. The officials started to ask me a lot of questions and continued by requesting me to follow them. I followed them to a room not far from the check-in counters. There I requested them to make a call for the person would be able to communicate better with them on my behalf. I then called Bob on my phone and gave the phone to the official I was with, but the official got annoyed while talking with Bob. She cut off the phone call and gave me my phone back. I was denying the situation I was in because I still had the hope that the authorities would let me go. At that moment they had just suspended me but later on they brought me to the narcotic board as they found nothing during their search of my belongings. Around ten o'clock p.m., a lady came in the room at the office of the narcotic board where I was waiting, and she asked me to follow her. As I had no option, I did as was requested. We entered another room. There she asked me to take off my cloths. At that instant I knew that it was over. I was so sad. While I was removing my clothes and the cocaine that was located outside of my body, I thought in myself: *"Here I am again, arrested again. What will I tell my family?"* Once finished, I gave all the items, clothes and drugs, to the official and she took the drugs with her and left the room for some minutes. Subsequently, the official entered the room, requested me to put my clothes on and brought me to the nearest hospital where the personnel made a X-ray photo of me. Because of the results, I had to stay in the hospital. I was put on a drip-feed and I stayed there for two days under surveillance of the personnel of the Criminal Investigation Department (CID).

A CID-officer handed me a Bible. He saw the expression of surprise on my face and went on to tell me that as he had heard me cry out to God, he felt in his heart to give me a Bible. Had I cried out to God? Yes, I had. When I was alone in the room, I cried out to God. Why, would be a good question. It was as if something in me knew that only God could help me. I appreciated this gift and from that moment on, I would have the Bible always with me even though I would not read it, at least in the beginning. I felt safe while having the Bible with me.

The CID-personnel were very nice to me. They treated me well and were so concerned about me although I did not deserve that. Once I had released all that did not belong in my body and the doctor's affirmed that I was sound and well, the CID-officials brought me to the Nima Police station. This police station is located in Greater Accra. The station was very crowded and noisy at the entrance and at the reception desk. The officials took me along to the section where the cells are and opened the door of one cell for me to enter. Ultimately, I stayed at the police station for a couple of weeks before moving on to the prison. While in the cells at the police station, I made some friends.

The first friendship was with two old ladies, aunty Comfort and Daavi. I would learn later on that they were deceived. They used to work as carriers for people who had bought stuff at the market in the town and would receive payment for their services. They transported stuff on their heads in big baskets. On a particular day, they got merchandise for delivery and the police stopped them for a random check while they were on their way to complete the delivery. As they had nothing to hide, they gladly cooperated with the check. Unfortunately, it turned out that the merchandise they were transporting contained forbidden items, including drugs. Therefore they ended up in the cell at the police station. I had just entered the cell when one of them gave me a scarf, told me that I should put it over my head, go down on my knees because they were about to pray. They surely prayed with power because I was immediately comforted. Once finished with the prayer, she washed my hands and told me that I should eat. I did as was requested. They had coconut and groundnut soup, something I surely didn't know from before. I thought that evening, so far, so good. Those were my first hours in the cells.

Days had gone by in which I had contact with Bob and he kept promising me that I would get a lawyer and that I would get out soon. In the meanwhile, Bob had arranged for breakfast, lunch and dinner to be brought for me, which in the beginning were always on time. Because of this gesture, I was convinced that Bob was concerned about my well-being. After some days, my lawyer came to meet me. His name was Kwami, a well-dressed and very kind gentleman. He came almost every day to see how I was doing and I was hoping that he would be able to get me out of the situation I was in. In the meantime that the lawyer was working on my case, I met a guy named Titus who was also locked up at the Nima Police station for the same reason, drugs.

He tried to have a chat with me, and though I had not given him any attention, he kept on being nice to me. At some point I asked him: "*What do you want from me?*" And he said: "*I want you to be my wife*". I told him that he could not be serious, not serious at all. I told him further: "*Number one, my situations is getting over my head. I just got arrested and you want me to be your what? Number two, I am 34. I am not a small child anymore, and then again I have five children. I am divorced because I cheated on my husband. So, please leave me alone!*" Then he said: "*Wow. Since you are conversing so passionately, I would like to know you better and in fact, I will also give you five children*".

I nodded my head and said in myself this man had either not understood what I had said, or he is crazy. As he saw the expression of unbelief on my face, he then said to me that he had a surprise. What a surprise it turned out to be!

He just got married to a nice university graduate student, his wife was pregnant for 3 months and he was very happy with her. After having received this information, I could not resist asking him: *"Why are you bothering me like this?"* He just said that I would not understand. This was the start of another friendship and we got very close as friends for the time that we had been in those cells. He gave me money and cared a lot for me. He also prayed a lot with me, that is why I am sure that he will be a pastor in the future.

*Moving on to phase two*

Some more days and weeks had gone by. Titus was transferred to cells at another police station and though he had given me a number to call if I would be in need, we had not spoken to each other after he had left the Nima Police station. I thought I was going home soon thereafter and therefore I did not bother to stay in contact with him. Sadly enough, the moment for me to leave the cells had not come after the transfer of Titus and I was there when his place was given to a lady called Philomena. She was also arrested for cocaine transport and brought to my cell. She was nice to me and she shared everything she had, from food to shampoo, with me. We both hoped that something would happen for us to leave but we could do nothing ourselves, we had to wait for our lawyers. My lawyer that used to pay me a visit in the beginning changed the strategy after a while and he went on sending a guy named Joshua instead. When Joshua came over to visit me, he would lend me his phone and I would talk to Bob who told me every time that I should not be worried because everything was arranged for. I heard the same message over and over till one morning my CID-officer came for me. I thought that they would release me because of the information that Bob continuously told me, so I was very happy and Philomena was happy for me. I was so happy that I called Titus to inform him that I would finally get out and that he should call me in The Netherlands when he gets out. I got indeed out of the cell at the Nima Police station but not to go home or something like that. Not at all. The CID-official took me to the Court and the judge gave me a remand in custody. My lawyer was not present at the hearing at the court-house; wasn't that strange? I was very disappointed however there was nothing I could do. Philomena and Titus were also disappoint-ed and they had lost all hope concerning my case. After the session at the courthouse, the CID-official took me to the Nima Police sta-tion to pick up the minimum stuff that I had there and then they brought me to my new accommodation.

The place where they brought me was called James Fort and you could see that the building was old, and you could recognize the slavery time in the construction and the artefacts. It was just like in the movies I had seen. When I entered, I was imagining how slav-ery could had been, how the slaves had lived in there. Tears flowed from my eyes because now I was there myself, in kind of a same situation as the slaves back then in the time that the Fort was con-structed and taken in use. What is it that God wanted to tell me? My mother is descendant of what people used to call the black peo-ple and my Father is descendant of the red Indians. My first long term imprisonment was at the prison in Peru, original territory of the red Indians and now I was in Ghana what is considered one of the original territories of the black people. I started to understand that God wanted to teach me something, but what? It was all a mys-tery to me.

*Dreams at James Fort*

Despite the little knowledge I had about God and surely little awareness of the greatness of God through His manifestations, I was to experience dreams with a profound meaning while I was at the James Fort. It is because of these dreams and the revelation that they contained that some inmates, and also officers, started to call me Pastor. To me it was just a way of saying thank you and I had for myself no expectations linked to the name. At that time I did not know the purpose God had for me in His Kingdom.

There at the James Fort, I met people praying and singing to the Lord while they were locked up in the cells. There I learned how to fast and pray, worship and praise the Most High. All of the aforementioned was mentioned to me on Curaçao. In Peru I learned a bit about it but it is in Ghana where after some time I went on to study it and practice it. I desperately wanted to go home and therefore I started to fast and pray together with the other inmates and as I did that, God started to give me some revelations. At first I could not understand it but bit by bit I realized that it was God talking to me or through me.

The second day at James Fort went without any particulars. I had the time to look better at my surroundings and prove more of the atmosphere. I went to bed that night with no plans or expectations for the next day. That night I had a dream. I dreamed about a prison officer who I had not seen so far. I saw in my dream how she held her hands even before I saw her face. Once I saw her face, I noticed that she was crying. Suddenly, I woke up. I took a look at the time, it was around 2 a.m. I did not understand the dream but I felt an urge in my heart to pray for this lady. I didn't really know how or what to pray at that moment, but I felt that I had to say something at least. I then decided to say: *"God, whatever is wrong with this lady, help her!"* After that I went on to sleep again and had no further dreams.

Despite the interruption of my beauty sleep, I woke up early. So, I was awake at the time the officers who had worked in the night went home and a new group of officers took charge. From where I was sitting, I could see the new group of officers installing themselves for the day. As my eyes slightly glided over the faces of the officers, as all were new to me, my eyes got locked on one face and I was astonished. I was amazed because in front of me, just some meters from me, I saw the person whose face I saw in my dreams a couple of hours before. I was asking myself how come I had dreamed with an individual that I had not seen before and how come I was seeing that individual in person after a couple of hours. Was it coincidence? I wanted to run to the officer and ask her all of these questions but I did not. I knew that the officers there were very strict and I was a bit scared to approach the officer. After a short while I took the courage and walked towards the concerning officer and said: *"Good morning Eraba"*. Eraba is the name that officers are called in Ghana. I continued saying to her: *"I dreamed about you last night and you were crying. I felt an urge to pray for you and I did"*. To my surprise, she only replied: *"At what time was that?"* I answered by saying: *"It was about 2 o'clock in the morning"*. The answer I got was something I had not expected. The officer went on telling me: *"Around that time I had a car accident, and my hand twisted but all of a sudden my hand became normal, like it had never twisted before. It was so strange. Now I know that it was your prayer that helped me out. God bless you"*.

As I watched the officer walk away, I started to realize that God works in peculiar ways. Maybe on that day I thought that the aforementioned experience would be one to never forget and one to never repeat. The reality is that it would repeat within 24 hours.

The following night, I dreamed again but this time my beauty sleep was not interrupted. This time I dreamed that another prison officer, who I had not seen yet, and she was complaining to me, that she and her husband wanted to by a white car but they are short of 1,000 dollars. I told her in my dream that God says that He will provide for you. The officers woke us up early the next morning for our workout session. While the other inmates and I lined up outside for the exercise session, the officer that would lead us took her place in front of the group, and as I got hold of her face, I realized that she was the lady I had seen in my dreams. Because of the experience of the day before, I felt confident of walking towards the officer to tell her about my dream. After the exercise session, I walked towards her, and told her: *"Eraba, you will get your 1000 dollars for your white car"*. The officer looked at me and she said to me: *"Who told you about my problem? Mind your own business!"* I did not feel offended or so and I replied politely: *"God said so. I dreamed about it."* After having said that, I just walked away being fully aware that the dream I had had was not just an inconsequential dream for the reaction of the officer made clear that the situation I had dreamed about was real. The officer came to me fourteen days later to thank me because indeed they were able to buy the car and it happened in an unexpected way.

When the news about these two situations was spread in the prison, some of the inmates and even some officers started to call me Pastor. On the other hand there were some who called me a prostitute. Only time would tell which of the two lifestyles would remain in my life. After the two experiences with dreams directed by God, I had a dream that was meant for me. This dream would be the start of phase three in my imprisonment process in Ghana.

### Phase three at James Fort

Time was going by and Joshua continued visiting me, though at a lower frequency than before. The day came that I had to appear before the judge again. The CID-personnel brought me again to court and this time the judge gave me a bail. The bail out amount was set at GHC1,000,000,000 (one billion Ghanaian cedi) which at that time was equivalent to about EUR 80,000 (eighty thousand euro's). The frequency of the visit of Joshua had become very low to none, but since he had told me that it would be okay, I kept on waiting for the day that I would be released. For the time being I kept on praying to God and fasting. Some weeks went by without dreams. Nine weeks after my initial experiences, I dreamed that I was brought to the main prison facilities in Ghana. I could not deny that God revealed to me that I would be sentenced. It was not what I was hoping for then again I knew I was guilty.

Short after the revelation provided by God, I met two other ladies from The Netherlands in the James Fort. They told me that both of them had pleaded guilty before the judge and they knew their final sentence and they would be soon moved to the female prison Nsawam.

I started thinking of my own situation and asked myself: *"What am I waiting for actually? Nobody comes to visit me anymore. So why wait?"* The next time the CID-personnel came to take me to the courthouse, I stood in front of the judge, I pleaded guilty for transporting 350 grams of cocaine and I got my sentence on the same day. It was on 3rd January 2007. Again I had no lawyer of flesh and blood to defend me. Despite the absence of my lawyer, the Court was gentle for me and ruled that my pre-arrest time should be discounted from the total time I was sentenced for. This was extraordinary as this was not common and had not been ruled for the other persons that were present that day before the Court. When I realized what had happened in the Courtroom, I had a big smile on my face. I had asked God to be my lawyer before the session in the Courtroom. The outcome of the session surely proved that God had answered my request.

> *"Mama, you are sick but God is going to heal you."*

After the sentence was made final, I went for one day to the police headquarters where my suitcases were stored and there I had the opportunity to call my sister and my daughter so that I could tell them that I was going to be in jail for almost ten years. My sister was choked and my daughter told me *"Mama, you are sick but God is going to heal you"*. At that time I did not understand what she was talking about. My daughter gave her life to Christ at the age of nine and all of us in the house thought she was crazy but, now I know she wasn't crazy. I am blessed with a daughter like her because through all the pains, she knew the Lord. I remember that she told me that when I went to prison the first time, she was one day sitting at the playground and crying, because she missed me. A small girl saw her. The girl walked towards her to ask her why she was crying and she explained what had happened. That little girl introduced her to Jesus and invited her to her church which was named Victory Outreach Church. From that moment on my daughter began attending this church and she even got baptized. Now that I know the Lord, I give thanks to Him for taking care of my family and I will continue thanking the Lord for taking care of my children even in my absence.

## *The real prison: Nsawam*

Once I had finished my calls with The Netherlands, I packed the little stuff that I had. One item that I surely took with me was a study Bible. There was a missionary from Holland that used to visit all inmates that were from Holland at James Fort. Her name was Colinda. While I was there, the missionary paid me a visit and brought me a big study Bible. It would take a while before I started making effective use of the study Bible. Once I was ready gathering my stuff, the CID-officials brought me to the female prison Nsawam where I would have to sit out my sentence. This was the start of the last phase in my process of being arrested in Ghana.

I arrived on a Saturday evening at the Nsawam female yard and when we walked inside, the guards searched my belongings thoroughly, brought me from one office to another. Then, they gave me an iron plate, a plastic cup and my uniform followed by my mattress and a wrapper. The next thing that I was allowed to do, was to take some of my own stuff and they brought me to the bathroom so I could take a bath. As I had my bucket from James Fort with me, the only thing I had to do was to fetch water. After this I was ready to take a bath. When I finished, I took my stuff and walked out of the bathroom. From there the officers took me to the place where I had to sleep allowing me to put my stuff and then they took me to show me the place where I would have to clean everyday till the day I would go home. When I returned to my cell I saw my friends from James Fort who were sent to Nsawam before me. They came to pick me up and show me the further way around. They gave me food and I had just finished eating when I heard the bell ringing. I went back to the cell that was assigned to me, cell 4.

The cells were rooms of 3 by 4 meters and often there were 55 persons in one cell. Around the last two weeks of December the amount of persons allocated in one cell could increase to even 62.

I was called by the cell leader, named Aunty Sara. We discussed the rules and regulations applicable within the cell. The next day, actually my first morning at Nsawam, I met a lady from Liberia, called Miriam. She was an Americo-Liberian. My friend from James Fort, Aunty Sara and Miriam had welcomed me in the beginning. They had been very good to me and provided for me later on too. Aunty Sara was very prayerful and every evening when we came inside the cell, she used to gather some of us together and gave us Bible studies and she also prayed with us. It was often so

interesting that I could not sleep afterwards. I remained awake processing the information received.

I would often think, will I stay here for 9 years? Will my children
make it without me? Similar questions came more than once into
my mind. I had no answer for those questions and I had to accept
that only time would tell.

## Forces in my life revealed

It was in this captivity that God made a path for me to start understanding that my decisions, life and foundations were built on the
wrong soil. As time passed by, I met and got acquainted with the
other inmates. There was an inmate called Toni who also became a
close friend of mine. She was a nice lady and was originally from
Detroit, United States of America. Throughout time I found out that
Toni believed in a lot of spiritual things. She went on explaining to
me that I had to pray and seriously if I did not, the witches would
destroy me. She took me to the back part of a cell where nobody
else was at that moment and she started praying in a way that I
considered very violently. I thought this woman was out of her
mind, really crazy and therefore I had not considered her remark as
a serious matter. She noticed my attitude towards her and her remark but she continued telling me that I should pray. As I still had
not considered her remark as important, I did not pray as fervent
and frequent as she wanted me to.

Toni told me once that few in that place, the Nsawam prison, were
from God, and that demons and witches were all around. I did not
understand what she was talking about till one day she told me that

I was a witch myself. She told me that in the morning hours and that day, I cried during the remaining part of the day. I cried because I had never heard such thing about myself before. You may think how it is possible that I was not aware of that. Let me just remind you that all I had done was what I had seen and experience since my childhood. Therefore to me, till the moment that Toni had spoken to me, what I had done before, was normal. My frame of reference for what is right and wrong was twisted since my childhood because of what I had seen my parents and grandparents do. This had influenced my life and the choices I had made.

In the week that Toni had spoken those harsh words to me, something happened that I would not easily forget. Despite the practices I had grown up knowing, seen and even executed myself, I had always thought that horror was only possible in a movie; thus it is fake. I was sleeping one night and at midnight a Romanian girl called Florin, who at that time was my cellmate, woke me up. I noted that she was very scared. I said to her: *"What is going on?"* She said: *"Look out of the window. Maybe I did not see well"*. I went to the window and looked outside and what I saw was like a movie. I saw a cat jumping out of the wall and the cat became a dog. I couldn't believe what I had just seen and I started praying to God and while praying I saw how the dog became bigger and bigger, like four times its original size, and then the face of the dog turned into a human face. I realized that indeed, the world is full of powers, good ones and evil ones.

The other inmates started acting strange towards me, from the moment that Toni had spoken the words to me that had contained a confrontation with my reality. The whole prison turned their back to me, as they had become aware of the words spoken by Toni to me. They believed immediately that I was a witch. I had a good relationship with a lot of the officers and the inmates said that I had charmed them; that was why I could have a friendship with them. The inmates even started to come together for fasting and praying against my evil powers. Sometimes they would walk towards me while they were praying and when they were standing in front of me, they would point their fingers towards me and start screaming *"Holy Ghost fire"*. As I understood later on, the fact that I used to sing the song 'I got the power', original of SNAP, made them think that I was singing and referring to the evil powers I had and not that I was singing a song just for singing, as a pastime.

There was an officer that had become a dear friend of mine. She was so dear to me and she helped me to pass through my time in jail. We used to fight a lot and then we would split up, not having contact with each other for a while and after some time, we would come back together. We had loved each other so much that it looked like we were a couple. It looked and felt like a husband and wife relationship. Our relationship was however not healthy. I felt like I could not be without her and she too felt that she could not be without me. Once I realized that the situation was not normal, I searched myself and I found out that I had wrong desires for this officer while this had never happened before in my life. I was a woman full of passion. The devil knew that.

Since there was no male around in the yard, the enemy of our souls had planted another wrong desire and thought in my mind. It is by the mercy of God that one day Toni, the same person that had exposed the wrong forces in my life, came to me and she gave me a book for me to read. The book was titled *Deliverance from demonic covenants and curses* written by Rev. James A. Solomon.

While reading the book I started to understand a lot of the things that had happened in my life. I also began to understand how to break the ties with the wrong forces on this earth. One of the things that I had learned was that you would have to face the hardship, and I was truly facing that in my life. The inmates who were my friend were not my friends anymore. My family was not interested in my well-being, and so on.

I also found out by reading the book that one could have a spiritual husband or wife and I began to understand the power of confession and deliverance. The information in the book made me start thinking about myself and the path that my life had taken. I really needed deliverance therefore I began to confess my sins to the Lord. I started feeling guilty and one day when I was in my cell, I said to God: "*I will not leave You alone until You deliver me*". Gradually, I was getting closer to God. It is after all of this that I understood that Toni had not lied when she had told me about the wrong forces that had been operating in my life. If I think about my grandmother and her actions, the places where I had been, my way of living and some more of that, the only conclusion that could be drawn was, that I was truly demonic possessed.

> *"I don't want to be like that anymore. God, deliver me from all this evil."*

My stubborn behavior could tell you that I had permitted for a lot of demons to enter and develop in me and on top of that, the marine spirit was playing its own role. What I mean with the later I will explain in chapter 8 where I will give an analysis of all the wrong forces that had been operating in and through me.

## My search for God

It was in those days that the inmates had turned their back on me, that I realized that I was alone; all by myself. If they were chatting, laughing or talking in groups and I went on to join them, just sit close by or say something, they would all get up and leave. If they were cooking, and see me passing by, they would put the lid on their cooking pots and whisper to each other that the witch is passing by. I was so lonely. I didn't know what to do. My family had also rejected me as no one was contacting me. So, I had to do it on my own. I was angry, bitter and sad. Where was the God they taught me to pray to? I didn't want to know nothing more about Him. Why was I in prison for the third time? Why did my family not want to help me? Why did I not hear from my boyfriend Carmelo? All of these were questions that I had. I felt that it was too much for me. I did not focus on what I had done wrong but on what others had done to me. Shortly after having this questioning sessions, I went on to my task which was sweeping in front of the doors of the church.

When I arrived at the location and was ready to start sweeping, I noticed that the chairs inside the church were disorganized. Instead of starting with the sweeping, I decided to go and arrange the seats inside. As I stepped inside the Church, it was like the sadness and bitterness took hold again of me and all I was able to do was throw myself on the floor. Once on the floor I started to cry. I cried from the bottom of my heart. This cry was neither for anyone to see nor for anyone to judge. It was between me and God. After a while I lifted up my head, looked towards the front of the Church and said: *"God if you exist, please tell me if I am a witch"*.

There sitting on the floor of the Church, I started thinking about my lifestyle in Holland and the things that I had done. The fact that I was married and still had affairs with other men; that I was with other people's husbands; that I used to smoke Indian hemp, and the fact that I was practicing voodoo including the bathing rituals so that I could succeed in trafficking cocaine. I realized that indeed I was a witch. The spiritual blindness was removed and I saw a bad me. As my mind was processing the information, I started to cry and this time more intensely and profound than minutes before. My first round of cry was because I felt I was misunderstood and left alone. It was a cry directed by self-centeredness. Now I was crying because of shame and repent for my sins. I cried out to God and I told Him: *"I don't want to be like that anymore. God, deliver me from all this evil"*. I felt a kind of relief in my heart. I knew that the process was not yet completed. This was just a beginning. After a while I was able to stand up and walked towards the door of the Church. Once outside I took my utensils and went through my daily routine.

From that day on, I started to fast and pray to the God I had come to know but still there was a lot more to be changed in my life before I could serve God as it should be.

*How I gave my life to Christ*

While I was living in The Netherlands, I attended church services but never with a heart for a search and an encounter with Jesus. If I had the right attitude and determination back then, God would have saved me years before. I attended the church at Nsawam from the moment I entered there. I started a real search for God as my mind was opened up for this as a result of 3 occurrences. These occurrences were:

· having read the book that Toni had given me,
· having repented while I was alone in the Church and,
· having understood from Whom salvation comes.

As I continued to fast and pray, I began to experience changes in my behavior, my way of thinking and feeling towards others and life in general. These were parts of my deliverance and healing process. The real trigger for change came after having read a passage in the book.

Sadly enough, I was one of the persons that Rev. Salomon had written about in his book. He mentioned in the book that some people do attend church services to worship God but they continue with their practices in and ties with the occult world. There in the Nsawam prison, I got the understanding of all that had happened to me in the past and I was determined to change, to work towards a change. In order to achieve change, I had to take action. One of the first steps was to attend church with an open and sincere heart.

I became more actively involved with the church and the church activities at Nsawam and soon the talent that God had given me, which is singing, was noted and I got the opportunity to join the choir. The choir was led by a lady called Aunty Camera. She was always leading in worship and praise in Ghanaian language during Church services or activities. I am a singer and singing is my passion. As I watched Aunty Camera during services, I wanted to have that role too, but because none of the inmates were talking to me, I did not know how to ask her about this. Nonetheless, one day I took the courage and walked up to her and told her that I wanted to fulfill the role that she has during services. Her reaction was to my surprise: "*Oh, you are the one!*"

As she saw the reaction of surprise and no understanding of her remark on my face, she continued: "*I had been praying about this because I am going home over two weeks and I had no successor.*" She taught me all that I should know in order to be able to lead the choir and in the following two weeks, I led the choir under her guidance. Though I was leading the choir, still none of the inmates would talk to me outside the Church building. I was still lonely. When I had nothing to do, I would go inside the Church and sit behind the drums. I never drummed in my life before so I was beating the drums without any coordination or rhythm. It sounded like *pang, boom, and boom.* After some trials and some ear pain, I heard a beat coming out that sounded more like the beats I was used to hear when I was performing with the bands in The Netherlands. Soon after I could drum almost as good as a professional drummer and from that moment on I would lead praise and worship and I would drum during church services.

As God was the one calling me to serve Him, the role I had within the church soon developed into the third in command for church matters and I also became the president of the Roman Catholics prayer group. Father Paul, who came from outside, taught me how to pray with the condemned prisoners. As I went through all of these experiences, I decided to give my life to Jesus Christ. There was a bible school, the Rabboni Bible School, of which the servants used to come inside the prison. Those servants helped me further with knowledge and understanding of God, Jesus Christ and the Holy Spirit. I was ordained by the Rabboni Bible School and from them I received, after completion of the first year, my 1$^{st}$ certificate and later on after completion of the second year, my diploma in theology. Another note about Rabboni Bible School is that at the time that I was released from prison, they offered me shelter. Furthermore, a special offering was requested on my behalf in order for me to cover the expenses for a plane ticket to The Netherlands. That was a tremendous help at that time, but before I reached that point, there was a lot more to go through between those walls.

While I was experiencing a spiritual growth in Jesus, I noticed that the troubles with my fellow inmates and even with the officers increased. I noticed that the battle was real as people didn't like me (anymore). I saw and even felt the jealousy around me and above all, the inmates were always plotting against me. I couldn't understand why it was always me, Bianca, to who they were appointing as the troublemaker and the guilty one. After a period of asking why to God and questioning the events that had taken place, I got the understanding that I was fighting against principalities and powers of the evil and not against the prisoners and officers as women of flesh and blood. There was something special about me that the devil also knew and saw. In order to beat the devil, which I had turned my back to by renouncing to my old practices and asking God for deliverance, I had to learn how to pray in warfare. Once I had learned how to pray in warfare, I saw how the hand of

God was moving in my favor. The troubles were solved one by one and slowly but steadily the inmates started to accept me back. I was again part of the group.

The other steps I went through that led to major change are extensively described in chapter 8.

## My visitors at Nsawam

Time had passed by and I had built up my routine within the walls. I was one early morning doing the usual things when Madam Vic, who was a high ranked officer, called me and told me that I should go to my cell and dress up because I had special visit. I had no idea what or who the visitors were and the only piece of additional information that I received from Madam Vic, was that they had a camera with them. I went to the cell to change and as I had informed my friends what was happening, they put on me an ice white top and a new blue prisoners uniform. When the other inmates saw my outfit, they started asking me: "*Where are you going?*" I told them, as I was told, that I had special visitors with cameras. The inmates, whom had been in there long before me, began laughing and mocking me, while saying: "*That is something you are wishing for because what you are telling now, cameras entering this yard? No, that has never happened before!*" I had not paid any attention to their talk and I kept on walking to the section where the offices were located.

The officer told me to wait on while she would announce that I had arrived. Soon she came back and asked me to enter and take a seat in the office of madam Araba who was the Officer-In-Charge (OIC) of the female yard. I was so nervous. I was sitting on a chair when the camera team entered the room. It was a relatively large group of visitors, especially for someone who had not received any visit since arrival at Nsawam. I greeted all of them and I noted that some were Ghanaians from TV Three and the tourists, being the very light-skinned people, were from TV station SBS6 from The Netherlands. After a short introduction, I was informed that SBS6 was working on a new program 'Gevangen in het buitenland' which means imprisoned abroad and they wanted to run my story as part of the program. The technician attached a microphone on my blouse and then the reporter asked me if I was ready for the interview. I said then that I was ready and the camera started rolling. The man asked me: *"Bianca, what happened?"* I told him what had happened before I had reached Ghana. Some more questions followed and after having answered all of his questions, I had the opportunity to sing a song and I choose to sing 'I am only human'.

After all of this, they had another surprise for me. The reporter asked me if I was ready to receive my sister. I said: *"Yes"*. The reporter continued asking: *"What would you tell her?"* I said that I would apologize to her and after having answered this question, they asked me to get up and my sister came into the room. She ran further inside and hugged me while tears were flowing over her face. Everybody around us was crying too. Once the filming session was over, I got some time to speak to my sister. She had also brought me pictures of my children where I could see how they had grown. The private time with my sister was not long but enough to tell her that I had changed, that Jesus had changed me. Every time when I look at my children I want to apologize to them for what I had done to them in the past and I pray that they will be steadfast men and women of God.

## The documentary

Colinda, the missionary from The Netherlands, used to come to Nsawam too. She came a few weeks after the recording of the documentary and she informed me that she got permission from the OIC to show the documentary, as this had run on the television in Ghana and in The Netherlands, to all inmates and officers on duty. The day and time of the presentation of the program was announced to the inmates and on the appointed day and time, a lot of the inmates gathered outside on the yard to watch the documentary. It was so touching.

The documentary started in The Netherlands at my sister's house where my sister and my daughters were interviewed. My sister had put on the CD where I was singing the song 'Pain' which I had written and was recorded by Ill Kid from Wolf Pack. That was the last group I was part of. On that CD there was also a song that I had recorded together with my oldest son.

The documentary continued with the moment when my daughters had brought my sister to the Schiphol Airport in The Netherlands. The following part showed my sister arriving in Ghana. She was brought to the Minister of Foreign Affairs and to the Dutch Embassy to get permission to enter the prison yard. The commentator mentioned that 3 days had gone by before they got an answer from the authorities. In the meanwhile they brought my sister to the James Fort for her to see where I stayed before I was moved to Nsawam. They brought her also to the Labardi Beach because of the waiting time. Though the site was wonderful, she was not able to really enjoy it as all she could think of was if she would get the permission to enter the yard or not. She also went to the courthouse and asked if she could do something about my sentence, but the officials told her that it was not possible and that 10 years was the lowest sentence that is given in such cases. The camera man had even filmed her standing under a tree in front of the embassy while she was crying. She was crying because she had realized that she would not see me for a long time. It was then that she met Colinda, who told her that she used to visit me, and that she liked me a lot. My sister went together with Colinda to the Mokola market and bought me lots of stuff.

Finally, the decision came from the authorities and my sister got the permission to enter the Nsawam female prison. The remaining part of the documentary was the part containing my interview and the moment my sister and I saw each other; surely, moments that I will never forget.

Once the video was finished, the inmates started to talk about it and some of them even expressed their feelings. A lot of emotions came out. Some even said that it was a lesson for them for when they get out, what they should not do wrong anymore. The Bianca on the film was another person than the one that got arrested and sentenced. What made the changes possible and how the changes were accomplished, you will read in the next chapter. What God has done for me, He can do that, and even more for you.

# CHAPTER EIGHT

# GO FOR THE CHANGE

I t took a long time for me to realize that I needed help. Not secular help, but the kind that only The Most High can offer. It is because of the help of God that I am a different person now. In earlier phases of my life, I was a very stubborn person and I never requested advice. If an advice was given to me, I would simply disregard it. I had to beat my head against the wall on every topic or situation, before I would accept or believe it. I was always incurring debts and could not control it. I was very careless with my things. I didn't know how to be neat and deliberately I dressed in ways to expose myself to others. I knew how to gossip very well and I was full of lust and passion. I was unfaithful, impatient and always restless.

That was then. Now, I am a different person and nobody, to be precise no human, helped to deliver me. In the process of change, I had to learn how to love myself and accept my wrongs. I realized, by the revelations received from God, that all the bad characters that I had, and I had shown, were demons. I was in a single word, possessed. Many people do not realize or do not want to accept that they are possessed. This might be your case too. If you study your actions then you know what you have been doing.

The bad characters you show, will allow curses to follow you without you being aware of it. You notice that things in your life are different or not going as it should be. You don't understand why everything becomes a problem or you don't understand the ways in which problems are coming on your path. These are all signs that you should scrutinize your actions. The following verses in the book of Romans are surely to be considered when thinking on your actions.

---

*For all have sinned, and come short of the glory of God (Romans 3:23).*

*Let not sin therefore reign in your mortal body, that ye should obey it in the lusts thereof (Romans 6:12).*

*For the wages of sin is death; but the gift of God is eternal life through Jesus Christ our Lord (Romans 6:23).*

---

While reading this book, you undoubtedly noticed that throughout the years, I had given opportunity to a lot of evil spirits to reign in my life. Some came from my ancestors, usually known as the generational curses, and some had the chance to enter my life by means of my own evil deeds. All of these curses came upon me. They followed the sins, or better said they were the results of sins.

The only way I could get rid of them was by repenting. The process for change starts with repentance. Then it is followed by fasting and praying to God Almighty. There is an essential element in this whole process. You must know what to repent from and which are the evildoers that must be cast out. In the following parts, I will tell you how I went through the process of change as described above.

## *My process of change*

The Scriptures tell us in Lamentations 1 verse 14: *"The yoke of my transgressions is bound by his hand; they are wreathed, and come up upon my neck; he hath made my strength to fall, the LORD hath delivered me into their hands, from whom I am not able to rise up."* In this Scripture reference is made to the word transgression. Transgression means wrong doings, disobedience, iniquities or lapses, and in the spiritual circle, it is represented by sin. Transgression is every evil deed, consciously or unconsciously, committed against one another as part of life's activities. It brings along demotion instead of promotion in the spiritual realm.

Romans 10:17 tells us that *"So then faith cometh by hearing, and hearing by the word of God."* It is only God who can solve your problem(s), and only true faith in the Word of God can guide you to your deliverance.

In my case, I prayed and fasted a lot in order to reach my deliverance. In prison there was no deliverance minister but God has given me power to tread upon the serpent, the scorpions and all the evil powers in the world (Psalm. 91:13). Based on these words, I believed that I could deliver myself, but in order to do so I had some tasks to complete.

First of all, I had to identify and classify the events in my life including my feelings and my thoughts. The second step was to confess the sins, repent and renounce to them.

The last one but certainly not less important, was to grant God the freedom to make me clean; make me a new person in Jesus Christ.

Below the list I had created for step one and some lessons learned regarding the points on the list:

1. Abortion.

2. Performing on and singing of fetish songs.

3. Sale, smoking, transportation and usage of drugs.

4. Sleeping with different partners. I was not happy in my marriage. I always felt that my husband couldn't satisfy me and because of that I slept with different partners. All of this led to impotence. Along the way of repentance, I learned that one can invite a spiritual husband or wife and all the odd consequences thereof. You can suffer hardships and go through time of poverty. Furthermore, marine spirits can make you experience dreams with Mammy Water.

   Mammy Water, also called Mother Water or Mami Wata in Africa, is a water spirit that is celebrated throughout much of Africa and specially the African Atlantic. Mami Wata is often portrayed as a mermaid, a snake charmer, or a combination of both. It is a host for other aquatic spirits which all honor the essential, sacred nature of water. It stands for sexy, jealousy, and beguiling which means highly attractive and tempting[2].

5. I executed fetish rituals when I was part of the cocaine business. This was done to guarantee that the authority would not disturb our plans. Part of the rituals was making sacrifices, throwing them into the rivers and also a spiritual bath. All these were tributes to water gods shortly said marine witchcraft.

6. My grandmother used to involve herself with spiritual parties, dinners and bath worshiping of ancestors. If I am not mistaken, every year the family had a family god celebration. All of this led to inheritance of curses. I know for sure that these brought problems in my marriage and different children from different partners.

7. My father was a womanizer and this curse goes on from generation to generation and does bring more curses with it.

8. Fornication, lesbianism & masturbation. All of these evil spirits had been tormenting me or working in me. I used to masturbate because I thought it was normal. But, this is also a part of Mammy Water, marine witchcraft. If you masturbate, demons will have sex with you. All the points indicated here can be categorized as religious sex.

---

[2] Smithsonian National Museum of African Art (n.d.), Arts for Water Spirits in Africa and Its Diasporas – Introduction retrieved from *http://africa.si.edu/exhibits/mamiwata/intro.html* on 17 August 2015

The consequences of the actions, or better said the sins, as described in the previous list were and are not limited to:

a. Crime related activities

b. Demonic strongholds partaking in my life leading me to many ungodly desires.
c. Idolatry. Spirits of Baal, Belial, and Jezebel influences leading to rebellion within the family.

d. Marital failure including hatred and divorce

e. Marine witchcraft related activities

f. Poverty

I had to recognize and confess all of the above as part of the initial steps on my route to deliverance. If down the road I had remembered a point that was not yet on the list, I would add it to the list because my goal was to reach a total deliverance of evil practices and spirits.

There was a time in my life that I was facing a lot adversary. On occasions I had even no idea what the cause was. When studying the Word of God, I began to understand some of the events in my life. Now I know that it all had to do with oppression curses. The Scriptures clearly tell us in Deuteronomy 28: 15-28 what the consequences were when the people privileged by God, had disobeyed God.

Furthermore, you can read in Jeremiah 11 verse 3: *"Tell them that this is what the Lord, the God of Israel, says: 'Cursed is the one who does not obey the terms of this covenant."*
In verse 10 and 11 it says further: *"They have returned to the sins of their ancestors, who refused to listen to my words. They have followed other gods to serve them. Both Israel and Judah have broken the covenant I made with their ancestors. Therefore this is what the Lord says: 'I will bring on them a disaster they cannot escape. Although they cry out to me, I will not listen to them."*

When you are disobedient to God, you are opening the doors for afflictions and curses. What you choose to do or follow makes the difference. If you don't know the Lord, the devil has the chance to rule your life. The only way to stop the devil, stop the effects of his actions and reverse his actions is with repentance and renunciation.

### Repent and renounce to the old

If you don't want to suffer again and remain heavy loaded, if you want solutions in your life, I want to introduce you to my dear Savior. He understands all your problems. Be aware that the devil will be mad at you and will try to destroy you. Then again, realize yourself that you will never be as low as you have been before, because Jesus is now at your side. When you put your problems and troubles at the feet of Jesus, He shall provide solutions. He always does. The devil is a lair and will always be.

If you are ready to leave behind the past and start with a new beginning, say out loud the next prayer:

*Dear God, I realize now that I was a sinner headed for eternity in hell. I know that because Jesus paid for my sins on the cross on Calvary, I can be forgiven. I can have peace with You. Today, I repent of all of my wrong doing. I renounce to the life of serving sin and myself. I ask You to grant me the gift of eternal life. I thank You that You have said: whosoever shall call upon the name of the Lord, shall be saved. Thank you that this promise counts for me too. I now understand Your mercy and Your love for me. God cover me with the precious blood of Jesus. Please send Your angels to protect me and let Your Holy Spirit guide me from now on in each and every decision in my life.*

Sign your name in the assigned section as a reminder of your decision and commitment to Jesus Christ.

Name, date and Signature:

If you don't know the Lord well or do not know what to pray for in order to reach your deliverance, the next paragraph will help you. In the next part I am providing some prayers points that can help break the yokes in your life and make you free to praise and worship our Creator.

*Prayer points*

It is only prayer that can help you break with the past and stay on the right track. Prayer and fasting really helped me so I want to share some prayer points with you. I know that the Almighty Father will deliver you as He delivered me from the enemy of my soul and of all his malicious army. You may pray for and with all of the following points or make a selection based on your situation. Be aware that you can pray with these points for another person as well.

Prayer points:

1. Every inherit yoke in my life, die by Holy Ghost fire.

2. All witchcraft links in my life, die by Holy Ghost fire.

3. You, spirit of lust in my life, die by Holy Ghost fire.

4. Blood of Jesus, disconnect my life from evil spirits in the name of Jesus.

5. Oh Lord, separate me from family and generational curses in the name of Jesus.

6. The marine power assigned against my life, perish by Holy Ghost fire in the name of Jesus.

7. You, spirit of setback, perish by Holy Ghost fire in the name of Jesus. I will go forward in the name of Jesus and never backwards.

8.  Blood of Jesus, disconnect my soul from the bondage of tradition in the name of Jesus.

9.  Every divination and witchcraft assembly going on against my life, cease by Holy Ghost fire in the name of Jesus.

10. Every power troubling my life, die by Holy Ghost fire in the name of Jesus.

11. Oh Lord, arrest every demonic spirit of failure against my prosperity in the name of Jesus.

12. My father and my God, I will be the head and not the tail in the name of Jesus.

13. Every pain in my life, cease by Holy Ghost fire in the name of Jesus.

14. Oh Lord, break every covenant between me and any demonic spirit now in Jesus name.

15. Each and every darkness in my life, receive light by Holy Ghost fire, in the name of Jesus.

16. Every stubborn problem in my life, receive solution by Holy Ghost fire in the name of Jesus.

17. Any dark power giving strength to my stubborn problems is destroyed by Holy Ghost fire.

18. Every family problem that has vowed to destroy me, be destroyed in Jesus' name.

19. Every seed of problem in my life, die by Holy Ghost fire in the name of Jesus.

20. You, stubborn problems disgracing my life, be consumed by Holy Ghost fire in the name of Jesus.

21. Oh Lord, let every disappointment be a blessing to me in Jesus name.

22. Oh Lord, let Your fire protect me and my family in the name of Jesus.

23. God of solutions, perform miracles in my life in the name of Jesus.

24. Oh Lord, I need my freedom. Grant me that by the power of the Holy Ghost in the name of Jesus.

Pray always with a sincere heart and let your prayers be accompanied by praise and worship, as praise and worship are the keys to open the gates of heaven.

*Last Comment and encouragement*

As a spiritual adviser, I, Bianca must warn you that the philosophies of this world lead to a death end. We must accept the word of God, which is written in the Bible, as the only immutable truth. If not, you will get lost in a maze and may never get back on the road that Apostle Paul spoke about to the Romans.

In Romans 10:8 is stated: *"But what saith it? The work is nigh the even in thy mouth, and in thy heart that is, the work of faith, which we preach."*

Furthermore Romans 10:17 says: *"so then faith cometh by hearing and hearing of the word of God."* The only power that I want to allow to control me now, is the power of God.

My dear brother and/or sister, I hope that you have learned a lot through this testimony. I am sure that as you were reading this book you were blessed. I pray in the name of our Lord Jesus Christ that your life may change for the better, amen. May God give you the ability to do the right things. May He grant you liberty, may His light shine on you and give you a glorious journey through life, amen. May the peace of God be with you now and forever, amen.

I was looking for love and I found the real love, Jesus Christ, who filled the emptiness in me.

# EPILOGUE

The basic text for this book was written by Bianca while she was at the Nsawam Female Prison in Ghana, Africa. Bianca received grace and was released from the Nsawam prison early 2013.

On March 3rd, 2013 she arrived at the Schiphol Airport, The Netherlands. After 7 years she was back in The Netherlands and was able to meet and hug her children and the other family members. Bianca's relationship with her mother and father had significantly improved compared to her experiences as described in the book. Her parents separated years ago but along the way God had been working in their lives too. They have improved their living circumstances for the better in the eyes of man and the Lord. Grandmother Cornelia passed away in 2010. Bianca was then imprisoned in Ghana and had not the chance to say farewell to her.

Bianca had learned her lessons from her past experiences and the grace that God had shown to her. Once in The Netherlands she was determined to make the best out of her life in the good sense and she started working for God. It was not easy. Though going through trials and tribulations she was able to stay on the right path and God continued to prove to her that He is a faithful God. Shortly after arrival in The Netherlands, she registered for a course as TV Presenter at TV College Hilversum. She finished the course with success.

Bianca had gained experience with presentation of programs as she had a program for Christian education running on the TV Channel Salto 2, which airs in the Amsterdam area.

Nowadays, besides work and taking care of her family, Bianca dedicates time to preach the Gospel and to motivate others to seek God. Bianca is a member and co-Pastor of the Ebenezer Church of All Nations in Amsterdam.

Her desire is to write a book about the experiences after being released from prison in order to encourage others and tell them that once God has delivered you, He will guide you. If it is the will of God, the aforementioned book, will become a reality as this one became a reality.

# WORD OF GRATITUDE

I want to thank my mother Orlinda Hoek-Westerveld, my recently deceased father Henry Grootfaam, my sister Mariska Grootfaam (La Queen), my children Chervino, Janice, Channelta, Chesteny and Margillio, and my ex-husband, father of my youngest children. Thank you for your patience throughout the years.

I also want to mention some dear one's who have helped me throughout the years: my late grandma Cornelia Westerveld (may your soul rest in perfect peace), my friend Romeo Babel, my prison mother Charity Araba Magnuse, Juiliana Mensah, Toni Warren, the Prison Ministry and all the churches who came to Nsawam Female Prison. Furthermore, Rabboni Bible School especially Pastor Dan Buxton, Pastor Franklin Amenu, Pastor Matthew Mba and his wife Gladys.
People I cannot forget are my best friend Zenabu Issifu, Diana Blijd, Florina Rotario and Angela Gils.

Highly Favored Publishing and Eunice Anita, thank you for all your help to make the dream of publishing this book a reality.

May The Almighty God bless you all.

# ABOUT THE AUTHOR

Bianca Grootfaam   is known in The Netherlands through the presentation of her case in the program "Gevangen in het buitenland" (Imprisoned abroad) which aired in December 2007 on the Dutch television station SBS6. She was born in Amsterdam, the capital city of The Netherlands, and has Surinamese roots. She is the mother of five beautiful children who she loves very much.

After an imprisonment in Curaçao, Peru and 7 years in Ghana, she returned to The Netherlands as a renewed woman that has encountered Jesus Christ. She lives in Amsterdam together with her family.

She has learned from her mistakes and wants to encourage others not to commit the same mistakes that she had made in the past.

# CONTACT DETAILS

For more information, counseling and prayers,

You may contact:

Pastor Bianca Grootfaam
The Netherlands
Email: bau3123@yahoo.com

Highly Favored Publishing
The Netherlands
Email: info@highlyfavored.nl